THE FULFILLMENT FORMULA

A Roadmap to Living and Leading with Purpose, Joy, and Authenticity

Melanie Crane

THE FULFILLMENT FORMULA

A Roadmap to Living and Leading with Purpose, Joy, and Authenticity

MELANIE CRANE

Copyright © 2024

All Rights Reserved.

No part of this publication may be reproduced, distributed, or transmitted in any form or by any means, including photocopying, recording, or other electronic or mechanical methods, without the prior written permission of the publisher, except in the case of brief quotations embodied in critical reviews and certain other noncommercial uses permitted by copyright law.

Disclaimer: The author makes no guarantees concerning the level of success you may experience by following the advice and strategies contained in this book, and you accept the risk that results will differ for each individual. The purpose of this book is to educate, entertain, and inspire.

For more information: Melanie@elevatemaine.com

ISBN (paperback): 979-8-9920674-2-2
ISBN (ebook): 979-8-99220674-1-5

Dedication

To my family and dearest friends, for never letting me forget the power within me or the unique gift I bring to this world and for reminding me to not take life too seriously. Your wisdom and love have been a calming and joyful presence in my life.

To my husband, Jasper. Thank you for showing me how to live authentically, boldly, and unapologetically real. You have given me the gift of unconditional love, providing space for me to grow and to make mistakes, and always believing in me. You have given me the courage to walk without fear and I love you so much!

To my mother for showing me the true meaning of integrity, kindness, passion and a joyful spirit. Your guidance has been the foundation upon which I stand. You taught me that no mountain is too high when approached with resilience, grit, and honesty.

To my coaches from my gymnastics days, for instilling in me the self-discipline, confidence, and mental strength to go after big goals and never settle for less. Your lessons have shaped me into who I am today.

To my closest soul sisters, for loving me fiercely and showing me what true friendship looks like. I am so incredibly grateful for each of you.

And to my spiritual mentors, for helping me gain a deeper understanding of myself and guiding me to transcend higher. You've challenged me to look inward, go deeper, and expand my truth. With all my love and gratitude, this book is for you.

Table of Contents

Preface 7

Introduction: Mantras and Morning Jogs 11

Chapter 1: Mirror, Mirror: Self-Discovery, Unfiltered 19

Chapter 2: Finding Harmony in the Hustle 33

Chapter 3: Find Your Purpose and Passion 49

Chapter 4: Discover Your HEART Goals 65

Chapter 5: Mental and Emotional Regulation 81

Chapter 6: Blasting through Ambivalence 103

Chapter 7: The Procrastinator's Playbook 123

Chapter 8: The Un-Niceties: A Guide to
    Embracing Your Inner Rebel 131

Chapter 9: The New Habit Manifesto 145

Chapter 10: Grit, Gratitude, Grace, and Finding Peace 159

Take the Next Step 169

Acknowledgments 171

About the Author 173

Preface

There was a time in my life when I believed that achievement, constant goal-setting, and striving for more were the only paths to fulfillment and purpose. I thought that my value, both to myself and to others, came from the answers I could provide and the success I could demonstrate. Like many of us, I got caught up in the idea that my worth was tied to how much I could accomplish, and I measured my impact by the outcomes I produced. But as time passed, I realized that this relentless drive came at a cost, often at the expense of my own peace.

This book was born from a journey, my own journey of self-discovery, shaped by both personal and professional experiences. It has been a path marked by challenges, triumphs, and a deep yearning to understand not just who I am but how I can help others uncover their own potential, their worth, and their confidence.

The calling to be a coach, a leader, and a teacher did not come to me all at once. It emerged gradually, shaped by the lessons I've learned and the transformations I've witnessed, both in myself and in those I've been privileged to walk alongside. Through years of education, hands-on experience, and personal growth, I've come to realize that my greatest impact lies in helping others remember the truth of who they are.

This work is deeply personal. It stems from a belief that the answers we seek are never truly outside of us, they are within. Yet, life has a way of clouding our vision. Fear, self-doubt, and the noise of the world can make us forget our strength and purpose. I've been there myself, searching for clarity, rebuilding confidence, and rediscovering my own worth. Every step along the way has reinforced my belief that transformation is possible, and that sometimes, all we need is someone to ask the right questions, to listen deeply, and to help us reconnect with what's already inside us.

What I aim to share in this book is not just theory or strategy but a heartfelt approach to empowerment and self-discovery. I want every person who reads these words to feel seen and heard, to find encouragement and inspiration, and to be reminded of the incredible power they hold. This is not about perfection or achieving someone else's version of success. It's about reconnecting with the desires of your heart and realizing that you already have what it takes to bring them to life.

The most extraordinary transformations I've witnessed didn't come from new information. They came from people remembering who they are. They came from clarity, confidence, and a willingness to lean into their unique gifts and capabilities. My role in those moments was simply to hold space, to ask the right questions, and to celebrate as they stepped into their truth.

Writing this book has been a humbling process, one that has deepened my gratitude for the work I do and the people I've had the privilege to meet. It's a reflection of everything I've learned, both from my own experiences and from the incredible individuals who've allowed me to walk alongside them.

This is not just a book about self-improvement; it's a call to remember who you are. It's an invitation to step into your confidence, embrace your worth, and pursue the life that's been waiting for you all along. I am honored to share this journey with you, and I hope these pages inspire you to see yourself in a new light, one filled with possibility, purpose, and unwavering belief in your own power.

May you find in these pages the courage to embrace your authenticity, the wisdom to lead with integrity, and the profound peace and abundance that arises when we unlock the power within ourselves, allowing our purpose, joy, and fulfillment to flow effortlessly.

Let's begin

Introduction
Mantras and Morning Jogs

In 2020, I decided to run a marathon. I spent most of my childhood and young adult years training as a competitive gymnast, but I was never a runner. I'm not built to like it, and it certainly doesn't come naturally to me. But I needed a mental toughness challenge, something that would tap me back into focus—refine my grit. So I decided to run.

You might wonder, *Why a marathon?* As a competitive gymnast who once had her sights on the Olympics, I have always craved a good challenge. And after fifteen years of competing, I needed something to lean into and challenge myself. I was so used to grueling days of six-hour training sessions and physical conditioning, attempting difficult skills on the uneven bars over and over again. But without that, I noticed that in some areas of my life, I was giving in, settling, and not pushing myself hard enough. So I did what any normal person would do: I signed up for a 26.2-mile run for "fun." Little did I know that it would be one of the best decisions of my life.

In the cadence of each step during my morning jogs, I found not only the heartbeat of physical endurance but also the steady flow of my thoughts. As the miles stretched out before me, so did the landscape of my personal and professional experiences. As I ran, amidst the monologue of my breath and the steady thud of my sneakers on the pavement, the idea for this book was born.

This book is not about running or elite gymnastics. It's about the lessons I learned through those arduous pursuits that helped refine and affirm what I already knew to be true about goal-setting, self-discipline, living with passion and love, motivation, and the art of focus and visualization. And simply the fact that our minds will give in far before our bodies do! I realized that if I packaged up everything I'd learned from my personal and professional experiences—as a collegiate gymnast, a cognitive behavioral therapist, a real estate broker, and a marathon runner—and shared it in the form of a book, I could make a massive impact in the world. My experiences, all tied together, have given me insights and perspective into how we as humans set colossal goals, achieve them, overcome failures and setbacks, and ultimately live abundantly and thrive in each area of our lives. We're not just talking about breaking old habits here; we're talking about releasing the mental and behavioral self-sabotage habits that lurk in the shadows of your life and business.

I wrote this book to give *you* the mental, emotional, and behavioral skills you need to take charge of your life and not only reach your biggest goals but soar far beyond them. All while enjoying the ride and living the depth and the width of each experience.

Introduction

This is a practical guide for go-getters, overachievers, and anyone hungry for abundance in every aspect of their life. What you are about to read isn't just a set of ideas; it's a framework and a process rooted in cognitive behavioral therapy and the science of habit formation. You will dive deep into your life's inventory, decluttering the psychological junk drawer, and stride forward with the swagger of someone who knows what they're doing.

At its core, *The Fulfillment Formula* outlines key pillars that will help you explore your true purpose and identify old self-sabotaging beliefs that no longer serve you then discover how to live life to your fullest potential. First, you'll take a good, honest look in the mirror to assess your strengths, desires, and limitations, and answer the question: "Who do I want to become?" I'll share my top routines and self-care rituals to help you stay on track with your goals and get in the right mindset to adopt new levels of self-discipline to achieve your goals without burning out. Then you'll dive deep into the discovery of your true purpose and passion, and learn how to set what I call HEART goals that are entwined with your very sense of self and who you want to be. You'll also learn the importance of mental and emotional regulation, and build new skills that will help you master the kind of self-awareness and self-control that will align how you think with how you feel—the ultimate superpower!

Ambivalence and procrastination can show up in all areas of your life, but you'll learn how to recognize them, trace these challenges back to their roots, and then use exercises and tools to blast through these roadblocks, giving yourself plenty of grace in the process. It's about progress here, not perfection.

You'll learn how to detox your life, embracing your inner rebel to let go of the constant pressure to shrink to fit what others expect of you. No more needing to be liked. No more subservience to societal "shoulds." You'll break free of the herd, detox your brain from its addiction to dopamine from our overstimulated society, and learn to stay on track to follow your bliss. Above all, you'll discover new freedom to express your true self.

Finally, we'll get to work identifying old habits that must die and embracing new ones guaranteed to get you where you want to go. What I found through self-reflection during my hours of running is that time and time again in my pursuit of excellence, I could not fail as long as I was stubborn enough to NOT give up. As I often say when I am coaching my real estate agents, you cannot fail if you do not quit. In order to have success in real estate, or anything in life, you have to commit to the long game—and if you are willing to buckle down, get clear, and commit to doing whatever it takes, success will follow.

You have everything inside of you to achieve what you desire, but it will take grit, perseverance, courage, and gratitude to achieve it. We also have to have fun and enjoy what we are doing along the way; otherwise we will burn out, feel uninspired, and lack motivation. It won't be worth the sacrifice if we do not love what we are doing while we are giving up so much to achieve it. For anything to feel like a success, we must love it and be in alignment with our path.

Introduction

The journey to anything worth working toward isn't a grand reveal; it's more of a gradual unfolding marked by hard work, perseverance, trust in the process of daily commitments, and a relentless pursuit of self-improvement. Spoiler alert: it's not always glamorous. Most of the time, it's a commitment to the unsexy work—a dedication to keep going, even when the only audience is your reflection in the mirror. We are not measured by how many friends we have, or how many likes and follows we get on social media. Life isn't a highlight reel of successes or a string of failures but more like a never-ending classroom, and learning from our mistakes, failures and lessons is the richest reward.

Like running a marathon, it all comes down to you against *you*. If you want to achieve greatness in anything in life, it is up to *you* to make it happen. Whether your idea of success is being the best partner to your spouse or being the number one real estate agent in the country, you will need a deep commitment to yourself and to the process of becoming the person you long to be.

As I learned during my months of training, running a marathon is an unwavering commitment to staying in the present moment. You can't get ahead of yourself. You just have to commit to one small step at a time and take your mind out of the pain of the moment. It's almost like suspending time, surrendering to something so much greater than yourself, and trusting that your mind is the only thing holding you back.

It's the same with anything in life, whether you're driving toward business success, or after something more personal like a fitness goal, a big creative project (like writing a book), or transforming your marriage. It is normal to feel a strong sense of motivation in the beginning to change your behaviors. But when motivation wanes, discipline steps in as the unwavering force to propel you forward. Forging a disciplined identity requires making certain aspects of our lives nonnegotiable. It's a transformative journey that demands a fundamental shift in how we perceive ourselves, an internal metamorphosis. Eventually, honoring our personal commitments becomes second nature.

When you're out there training for your "marathon"—literally or figuratively—success or failure comes down to your integrity to follow through on your commitments. When the road seems unimaginably long and you feel lonely, exhausted, defeated, and in pain, I don't want you to throw in the towel and make excuses for why you never followed through. If you give up on what you started, you can probably come up with a million reasons why you quit. But how do you find the mental, physical, and emotional strength to keep going? *That's* what this book will show you.

Our purpose, I believe, is truly to live out our greatest potential as human beings in every way possible. And only YOU know what that looks like. That is the beauty of life. Running your own race is a beautiful journey of self-discovery, with each step getting you closer to an energetic alignment with all that you are meant to become. One step at a time, one day at a time, one action at a time—one thought, feeling, and belief at a time.

Introduction

So, are you ready to set the world on fire? Is there a purpose bubbling within you, waiting to break free? If you're up for some heavy lifting (of the mental and emotional kind), ready to commit to the magic, and ready for radical improvement, then you picked up the right book. We're not just putting on our sneakers; we're strapping on rocket boosters for the marathon of mind and achievement. The starting gun has fired, my friends. Let's dive into the wild, sweaty, exhilarating journey together. Lace up, because we're about to sprint toward your best life!

Chapter 1
Mirror, Mirror: Self-Discovery, Unfiltered

Up until recently, I spent most of my life on autopilot. How I would think, act, eat, drive, work—I operated on fast-forward, impatient to get to the next thing just to "finish it." My whole life was so structured that I became wired to just check things off and move to the next task with little awareness, or true fulfillment, for that matter. That constant internal pressure did not allow me to take time and actually learn something, enjoy a meal, or just be intentional with my tasks.

That kind of unconscious, autopilot tendency caused extreme cycles of burnout, total exhaustion, mistakes at work, and deep dissatisfaction. Around the time that I began to write this book, I reached a point where I felt I couldn't escape the pressure I had created in my life. The drive I learned from a young age in competitive gymnastics had evolved into such an extreme form that I suddenly found myself wanting to shut everything down, sell my business, and move to Puerto Rico, a place where my husband, son, and I feel such a sense of peace and the ability to escape from the pressure of life.

But after some self-reflection, I realized the solution to my anxiety didn't have to be so black-and-white. I discovered something useful: maybe I already had within me everything I needed to find that peace and joy I was yearning for. By slowing down, resting, playing more, creating more balance in my life, and not working so hard, I could create the happiness I longed for. But I was fearful of letting go of the parts of my personality that had seemingly brought me so much success (i.e., my competitiveness, determination, and extreme drive), especially because of my industry. Real estate is competitive by nature, and I was afraid that slowing down would make me lose my edge. That's when the irony hit me. If I was willing to give up everything I'd worked so hard for and move to Puerto Rico, why was I so unwilling to change my approach to life instead?

It was time for a good, honest look in the mirror. It was time for radical honesty about how my past had shaped me, in good ways and perhaps unhealthy and outdated patterns of behavior, and what it means to give up my old way of approaching life that had caused burnout, depression, and the sudden need to escape everything. As someone who is highly competitive and "gold medal" driven, this insight brought up a lot of fear, but it was suddenly so clear. Peace and serenity are found from within. I was determined to create my inner sanctuary, and then share what I've learned so that you can find peace, joy, and happiness too while on the road to success and achievement.

Chapter 1

Take an Honest Look in the Mirror

Self-awareness requires you to peel back the layers and face your true self, in all your unfiltered glory. It requires a trip back in time to look at your past, and radical honesty about everything you need to let go. Yes, it can be difficult to take that hard, honest look in the mirror, but imagine the freedom of being able to let go of everything that doesn't serve you!

Happiness is an inside job. And self-awareness is the GPS for the soul. Self-awareness is the compass that guides us on the intricate journey of living a fulfilling life and achieving our goals. It involves a deep understanding of our strengths, weaknesses, values, and motivations. With this introspective clarity about what lights us up, inspires us, draws us in, or creates internal resistance and unhappiness, we gain the ability to set authentic and meaningful goals that resonate with our true selves. Through self-awareness, we navigate life's twists and turns with purpose, aligning our aspirations with our core identity.

Self-awareness is truly the cornerstone of personal growth and development. Knowing ourselves enables us to recognize and break free from beliefs that hold us back, and fosters resilience in the face of challenges. As we define our understanding of who we are, we cultivate a more profound connection with our goals, making the pursuit not just about external achievements but an internal journey of self-discovery. A fulfilling life emerges from the fusion of our aspirations with authenticity. Self-awareness serves as a catalyst for fulfillment in every part of our lives.

Take a Personal Inventory

Grab a sheet of paper and your favorite pen and do the following: Conduct a purposeful examination of every part of your life, from your relationships and career to your personal values, finances, dreams, and well-being. On a scale of one to ten, rate your satisfaction in each facet. Reflect on the following questions:

- What do you feel you're exceeding at, and where could you improve?
- Is anything missing from your life, and does your inventory include anything you'd love to just let go?
- What would cause the number in that category to increase? What would need to change to move that dial?
- What is getting in the way?

This type of thorough assessment allows you to discern what activities, traits, and habits align with your aspirations, and what you may need to change. This clarity will empower you to acknowledge your accomplishments, identify areas for growth, and reassess your priorities. Whether you are evaluating the quality of your connections, your career satisfaction, or your emotional well-being, a holistic personal inventory will become your blueprint for intentional living. You'll be better able to make decisions and know which actions to take and what you can let go so that you can live a balanced life.

If you rated something on your inventory a seven out of ten, don't just shrug that off. Interrogate it like a detective at a crime scene. Where are the wheels on the bus of your life falling off? Ask tough questions. Be radically honest. This exercise is for you alone, and there's nobody to impress. It takes courage to face the potholes head-on, but the reward is a life of fulfillment, peace, and joy. You can do this!

The Power of Radical Honesty

People who have not truly done the work of self-honesty are often living the dreams of other people without any conscious awareness. They are in jobs they hate and relationships that are unhealthy and unfulfilling, often experiencing some form of depression or anxiety stemming from the fact that they are not connected with their truth. These people might be jealous and competitive, stuck in an unfulfilling cycle of trying to prove themselves because they truly do not know who they are.

Radical honesty in the context of pursuing life goals is a commitment to transparent and authentic communication with yourself and others. It involves peeling back layers and dismantling the barriers of pretense with a sincere desire to explore your aspirations and challenges. When you do this, you gain a profound understanding of your desires, strengths, and limitations, which sets you up to move forward in the direction of your true integrity.

This type of radical honesty serves as a powerful tool for building connections and collaborations too. When we openly share our ambitions, setbacks, and intentions with others, we create a supportive environment where our collective efforts align with our aspirations. This type of radical honesty strengthens our integrity and also welcomes constructive feedback from people we trust. I have found that being my authentic, perfectly imperfect self allows other people to be real as well, which fosters much deeper connections with the people we care about most. For example, I have an incredibly deep, loving, and supportive relationship with my husband, and it stems from our commitment to be radically honest with ourselves and each other, day in and day out.

Complete the Unfinished Work of Your Past

To live abundantly and thrive, you must first understand where you are now and how you got here. What life experiences created the habits, traits, and outlook you have today? Before you can get to the heart of your true purpose and create the roadmap to live true to your calling, you have to look at your unresolved problems, messes, the things you feel guilty or ashamed of, past wrongdoings, and your current circumstances. To be the master of your fate, you must complete the unfinished work of your past.

Go back to the beginning of your story, and think about the pivotal moments and experiences that shaped you. But before you dive too deep into what might be painful past experiences, remember this: **you are NOT broken**. I've spent so much of my life searching for ways to fix what I felt was broken so that I could heal myself and deepen my awareness. I don't regret the time I spent learning and evolving, but what I've realized is that when we accept the fact that we are not broken—that

Chapter 1

the divine essence within ourselves is untouched—we can release the search to heal and fix the parts of us we don't like. Anchoring into our truth about who we are originates in the quiet space within our heart where we can bask in what we recognize, and release the egoic part of us that thinks we need to be fixed.

I'll go through this exercise with you and share my story and what I discovered in my own mirror exercise. I'm still uncovering layers that show up in my life today.

For me, everything that shaped who I am today began when I was seven years old. After my parents' divorce, my mom moved me and my brother from Philadelphia to a small town in mid-Coastal Maine. My brother and I had a hard time adjusting to the move and the divorce, and it soon became clear that I needed an outlet. My mom signed me up for gymnastics, starting with one class a week. I soon fell in love with the sport. I loved the challenge, I loved my coaches, and most of all, I loved the friendships I developed.

By the age of ten, I was going to gymnastics several times a week and quickly rose in levels. At the age of twelve, I convinced my mom to let me move back to Pennsylvania to live with my dad so that I could train at the Parkettes National Gymnastics Training Center in Allentown. Moving away from my friends and family was the hardest decision I ever made, but I wanted the opportunity to train at the Olympics facility. The demands of my gymnastics schedule and homesickness were almost unbearable at times. I was training six days a week, five to six hours a day with regular weigh-ins. The pressure was crippling, and my loneliness never went away. After achieving the status of a Level 10 Gymnast—the highest level before becoming an elite competitor—I decided to move home.

I knew that my last years of high school were pinnacle years for college recruiters and applications. I received letters from several Division I universities hoping I would compete for their gymnastics team. At my prequalifying meet for Nationals in my junior year, I was under an extreme amount of pressure to perform at my best, as many college recruiters were watching me. I struggled with performance anxiety and would often make careless errors during competition or overthink a skill I had performed hundreds of times in practice. When it was my time to step up to the uneven bars and perform my routine, I completely crumbled under the pressure and couldn't finish my full routine. That moment when I stepped off the mat to salute the judge is still difficult to talk about. The defeat was crushing. It was the moment I gave up my dream to go to Nationals and compete among the nation's best gymnasts.

For several days after that devastating performance, I couldn't go to school and could barely function. It felt like every moment and every hour in the gym over the eleven years leading up to that moment was shattered. I decided to make it my life's purpose to understand the human mind, so I could understand what had happened to me that day. I went on to earn a bachelor's in psychology and a master's degree in clinical social work, specializing in cognitive behavioral therapy and EMDR (which stands for eye movement desensitization and reprocessing). I opened a private practice to work with youth and adolescents who had experienced trauma, depression, and other mental health issues, as well as elite athletes on peak performance anxiety. I felt it was my mission to help other athletes like me, who struggled with mindset and confidence but had the heart, the work ethic, and the dedication of any Olympian.

Dedicating oneself solely to one goal or pursuit can be a blessing and a beautiful journey, but that kind of singular focus can also be the most devastating experience a person can have. That day at Regionals taught me a lot about the importance of enjoying the journey without being so attached to the outcome. If we're focused only on the outcome, if it doesn't quite happen the way we expected it to, the experience can be crushing. And we miss all of the other wonderful experiences and lessons that shaped who we were in the process and pursuit of that goal.

I carried that lesson with me into my private practice, and later, when I started to look for a new career opportunity that would provide me with more challenge and opportunity to impact more individuals, and provide a greater path to personal and professional abundance. Through prayer and meditation, I felt called to pursue a career in real estate. I loved the idea of putting my work ethic to use to create my financial future without limits and support and coach highly motivated agents to achieve their goals.

My first year as an agent was rough. I spent three hours every day cold-calling, knocking on doors, and doing anything I could think of to succeed. I was too proud to ask my fiancé at the time for gas money, so I cold-called until I landed my first buyer, then my second, and so on. To be honest, my only goal in my first year was to make enough money to pay for an open bar at my upcoming wedding. With hard work, relentless pursuit, and clarity, I sold twenty-seven homes and more than tripled my income from my previous profession as a licensed clinical social worker. Needless to say, we threw one hell of a party at our wedding!

I went on to become an assistant team leader for one of the largest and most profitable market centers in the world, and within eight months, I'd recruited over 120 agents to our company and gained massive clarity about my next step, which was to launch my own real estate brokerage. As I write this book at the start of summer 2024, my business partner and I have launched our brokerage, Elevate Maine Realty, with a mission to revolutionize the industry and elevate the experience and success of our clients, our agents, and our community.

Gymnastics has also imparted significant life lessons that I carry with me. The sport's demand for excellence ingrained in me a relentless pursuit of goals. Setbacks are merely opportunities to grow, and failure and quitting are simply never an option. Even today, gymnastics remains a huge part of my life, constantly reminding me of the strength and perseverance that lie within me. The discipline and mental fortitude I developed as a gymnast continue to drive my ambitions, making me who I am today.

Chapter 1

Over time, I've learned to stop operating from a place of effort and force, and to surrender, knowing the universe has my back and trusting that my needs will always be met. First, I had to get clear on what my boundaries and needs were. Then I had to learn to trust myself to have the strength to honor those boundaries and needs in any setting, no matter what. I've had to learn to speak up in situations I don't agree with and to speak with power instead of being the peacemaker. If I have something to say or feel uncomfortable in a situation, I'm not afraid to rock the boat. Every time I listen to the silent whisper of my own needs, I rebuild trust in myself. But I couldn't do any of these things until I went down the path of self-discovery that I'm asking you to walk now.

Here's something else I discovered: I was so disciplined with my gymnastics training that I don't recall a time when I allowed myself to be carefree and playful. As far back as I can remember, I had to take life seriously, and I built defense mechanisms to protect the fearful little kid I still carry within me. That fear has often kept me from being who I am and being okay with people seeing me for ME, not an image of perfection. Only recently, through my morning meditation on my self-healing journey, have I been able to release that little kid within me and finally let her go play. If I lose it all because I'm no longer killing myself to achieve it, then it's okay, because I was willing to walk away from it all anyway.

Go Back to the Beginning of Your Story

Now that I've laid bare my story, it's your turn to take an unfiltered journey of self-discovery. What lessons did you learn, and what shame, guilt, and self-doubt do you still carry with you because of things that happened in your past? What's no longer serving you? What characteristics or traits did those experiences instill in you that you can rely on when you need them?

To help you pinpoint things that give you strength and things that might be holding you back, try asking for feedback from a trusted friend or partner, without getting defensive when they answer honestly. "How do you perceive me? Are there any blind spots I should know about?" These kinds of questions give you insight into your strengths as much as your weaknesses and help you zero in on what you can let go of and where you can improve as a partner, colleague, individual, and professional. It's like crowd-sourcing wisdom—a focus group to help you move forward to your dream life with your eyes open, fully aware of what brought you here and how to get where you want to go.

Again, when you look in the mirror, you won't love everything you see, but facing this type of radical honesty allows you to clear your side of the road, so to speak, so that you can move forward without any distraction, resistance, or baggage from the past. It allows you to let go, accept yourself as you are, and move forward in full alignment to focus on your future without constantly being nagged and pulled backwards by the inner voice in your head. Self-discovery is a chance to improve your storyline. Who doesn't want to do that?

Chapter 1

I've spent most of my life looking for external validation and external answers from books, teachings, and other people to hopefully give me the peace and happiness I deeply desired. But finally, I realized those things were already within me. They had never left! When you realize that, you stop searching for ways to end your emotional suffering and fix what is not broken. You find happiness and peace where it never truly left.

I was ready to give up everything just a short time ago, until I realized that I was actually just searching for peace and serenity in the here and now. Think about your life and situation. If you could sell everything and move away to a tropical paradise, would you do it? If the answer is yes, then I bet you're also willing to give up everything that no longer serves you—to change your approach to life and make room to rest and play—so that you can find peace and serenity within you right now, no matter your circumstances or challenges, and carry it with you on your journey to fulfillment.

To reward you for this hard work, the next chapter is all about taking care of your physical, mental, and spiritual health. It's like a trip to the spa—get ready to nourish your body and soul and get yourself in the right mindset for everything else you'll learn in this book. By the time you finish reading, you'll have everything you need to achieve any goal without burnout.

Chapter 2
Finding Harmony in the Hustle

In the pursuit of a highly successful, fulfilling, and impactful life, the key lies in the mastery and daily recommitment to the basics. What our bodies and minds need to thrive is actually quite simple, yet we find ways to overcomplicate it, as we tend to do with almost everything else. These basics, often overlooked in the hustle of modern life, include the foundational pillars of mental and physical health: a balanced diet, regular exercise, spirituality, and ample rest. Never underestimate the power of rest! Any athlete will tell you that skipping adequate rest guarantees failure in the long run.

To truly master the basics, we have to commit to it like a full-time job. Taking care of yourself is an investment that pays dividends across all aspects of your life. Every morning, without fail (ask my husband), I wake up before my family, drink a tall glass of water, pour myself a cup of coffee, and before I check in with the rest of the world, I check in with myself. I pray, meditate, visualize, journal, and recommit to my goals and how I need to approach my day. I have not missed my morning routine since I was thirteen years old and living in Pennsylvania, working toward an Olympic dream.

Mastering the basics is not just a life hack; it's the secret to a world beyond mere existence. When things feel out of control in my life, I have always known how to get back on track by just focusing on the basics. Sometimes a quick workout or recommitting to my daily time block gives me enough sense of control within myself to get back on track and create that positive momentum for my day ahead. Let's look at how you can get started mastering the basics.

Start with Simple Routines

The first step is to set up routines and habits that help you stay on track every day. Daily commitment to personal well-being is my "morning coffee." It's nonnegotiable and essential for a kick-ass day. My morning routines have been the cornerstone of my life that I haven't just *lived* but *curated*, with purpose and connection that has had an invaluable positive impact on my self-worth and overall well-being, personal relationships, and career goals. My morning routine is when I reconnect with myself and recenter. Without this time, I would be less productive, less focused, less patient, and less able to handle challenges and relationships throughout the day with grace and love.

I highly recommend you develop a morning routine, because before you can take on the world, you must find the wonder in grounding yourself in gratitude, in setting intentions for the day, and in visualizing the impact you want to make. This is your sacred time that no one can take away. Carve out a small corner of your house and curl up with your journal, coffee, and a warm blanket. This time of clarity, quiet, and deep introspection is the most important time of your day. Lately, my morning mantra has been:

> I am grounded in my truth.
> I am centered in my power.
> I am humble, yet strong.
> I approach this day with clarity and grace.

The Power of the Right Mindset

Next to my morning routine, the most important contributor to my success has come from a relentless pursuit of mastering my mindset. As a competitive gymnast, I learned early on the power of the mind on our overall ability to function in a world full of chaos and distraction. Learning how to focus was the biggest gift my gymnastics career gave me for lifelong success. Gymnastics is a sport in which you can get severely hurt if you lose concentration for a split second. At a young age, I developed the ability to dial it in and shut out all other distractions. Including the distractions of negative self-talk, fear, or any other emotion that takes you away from the life you want.

Mastering your mindset takes continual work. After my struggles with performance anxiety, I learned everything I could about how to overcome mindset challenges that can hold us back if we don't learn how to focus and move forward, even in the face of powerful fears or damaging self-beliefs.

It starts by truly understanding that you have the power to create the life you want—the relationships, success, feelings, and connections—by simply *deciding* to feel the way you need to feel to achieve what you want.

We are the curators of our lives. This is the most powerful realization I have ever had, and when you embrace this truth, it makes life so much fun! If you choose to believe otherwise, you will notice the many instances where you can fall into a vicious cycle of victimhood. Or you can choose to harness the power of empowerment and decide how you want to feel, just by shifting your perspective. Ultimately, this powerful shift will bring you huge results.

Affirmations and setting daily intentions reinforce focus, gradually transforming into habits, and ultimately becoming ingrained in your character. This intentional approach safeguards against the unconscious development of reactive patterns that may emerge during daily interactions.

Embracing affirmations can be a powerful tool to align yourself with positive energies and foster personal growth. Affirming *I am joyful and happy with who I am and who I am becoming* sets the tone for self-acceptance and continuous evolution. Expressing gratitude through affirmations such as *I am in full appreciation for all that I have* cultivates a mindset of abundance and contentment. Standing on the brink of future possibilities while embodying feelings of eagerness, ease, and optimism—as stated in the affirmation—propels you toward a state of anticipation without succumbing to impatience, doubt, or unworthiness. These affirmations encourage you to openly receive a state of well-being and creative thought.

The significance of setting daily intentions cannot be overstated. This is how you align your conscious and subconscious mind, and over time, you'll find that you have begun to create a reality that aligns with your positive intentions. At first, you might have to work at this, but eventually, the process of taking action that aligns with your desired outcome will start to happen on autopilot. We already operate on autopilot for a significant portion of our day, which is why being conscious of our habits is so important to avoiding patterns that lead to unintended outcomes. I often carry around a notepad with my affirmations and intentions for the day. By doing so, I'm trying to reaffirm in my mind until my behaviors and habits start to reflect those affirmations. There are so many distractions in this world, so solid affirmations are like anchor points, blocking out the hustle and busyness of the world around us.

When it comes to mindset, you must learn to delete everything from your mind that doesn't move you forward, which is why we started with a radically honest look in the mirror. Now that you've cleared the clutter from your soul, you can make space for the goals that truly matter.

Take Care of Your Physical Health

In the demanding world of competitive gymnastics, where precision and strength intertwine, the well-being of my physical self serves as the cornerstone for success in every facet of my life. Since I was a little girl, I would go on fifteen- to twenty-mile bike rides with my dad. He taught me that by strengthening our bodies, we strengthen our mindset, our will, and our ability to commit to and stay focused on tasks. The connection to our mind and body is profound. Confidence, happiness, relationships, energy levels, mental clarity, and the overarching discipline required to become the best version of ourselves all hinge on the foundation of a well-tended body. So if you truly want to identify as a self-disciplined person or simply want to strengthen that muscle, start with your health. Take care of the most important asset you have—your body—and everything else will build from there.

Nurturing your physical well-being is self-care in its highest form. When you recognize the symbiotic relationship between body and life, you also realize that success in any area of your life starts with good nutrition, sleep, and exercise. Your physical health routines become a sanctuary that you always have control over. Think of it this way: the pursuit of anything worthwhile in life demands discipline, and the body, as the vessel carrying us through this journey, requires no less attention than any other goal we aspire to achieve. In my experience with setting and achieving goals, it is not feasible for me to declare myself a "disciplined person" while neglecting my physical health.

This is where self-honesty and integrity come into play. Now is a good time to take stock of how you take care of your physical health. The good news is that if you're not happy with your current habits, you can change that right now! To manifest our best selves in the broader spectrum of life, we must first prove our dedication and discipline in the microcosm of physical well-being. Anything less is a disservice to the authenticity we aim to embody. The path to success isn't just an outward trajectory but an inward journey too. This is your chance to improve every part of your life, and every act of self-care is like putting another deposit in the bank. Our bodies are the vessels that carry our dreams, aspirations, and potential for greatness. I never said it was going to be easy, but every act of self-care will pay off in huge dividends.

Motivation versus Self-Discipline

What is the difference between motivation and self-discipline? Put simply, motivation is our desire to pursue a goal. It's the reason we keep taking action to get where we want to go. We all experience varying levels of motivation—we're human, after all. We can always find a million reasons why we can't do something or haven't gotten around to it. That's where self-discipline comes in to save the day.

Self-discipline is our ability to regulate our thoughts and emotions in pursuit of a goal, even when we want to throw in the towel. Self-discipline takes over when motivation isn't enough to keep us moving. But we still have to be careful to balance our energy to avoid burning out.

I have struggled with this for a large portion of my life. Whenever I feel tenacious about a goal, I attack it with intensity for a short period until I burn out. I've learned to slow down and try to approach goals and tasks with a more balanced energy. Instead of cycling through intense spikes of effort followed by dramatic drops in motivation, I'm able to balance my energy for long-term progression.

So how do you find that balance? First, try to remove emotion from the equation. The trap we all fall into is waiting for the right time to feel "motivated enough" to perform a task or activity. The reality is that there will never be the perfect time to execute. To avoid that trap, you must simply remove the emotion and move forward with intention and purpose, DESPITE how you feel about it. This requires a strong sense of self and the ability to keep your emotions between the guardrails. I've devoted a whole chapter to mental and emotional regulation later in the book, which will help you master this vital life skill. But a quick trick I have found helpful for finding motivation quickly is the 5 Second Rule, a phrase coined by international speaker and well-known author Mel Robbins. Whenever you're faced with a task you're resisting, don't think and don't pause; just give yourself a five-second countdown, and then take action!

But remember, if you are feeling unmotivated and finding it very difficult to get yourself to do what you know you want to do, don't beat yourself up! Shame doesn't help; it only creates more resistance. If you can't find the motivation or the discipline to take action, ask yourself the following questions from a place of curiosity and not judgment:

1. Am I sleeping enough, and fueling my body properly so my brain is operating at its highest level?
2. Am I enjoying what I am attempting to do? Why, or why not? If not, what needs to change so that I find more excitement in the task in front of me?

3. Does my mindset support my mission? Why, or why not?
4. Do I have an accountability partner to help me? Who is my support system for this goal, and how can I tap into that support more?
5. Do I just need a vacation?
6. What part of me is resisting? Do I need to modify my goal in this season of my life? Have my priorities changed?
7. What small incremental step can I take today that will move the dial and spark motivation?
8. Have I stopped to celebrate my small wins enough?

Spirituality

In her book *Rising Strong as a Spiritual Practice*, Brené Brown says, "Spirituality is recognizing and celebrating that we are all inextricably connected by a power greater than all of us, and that our connection to that power and one another is grounded in love and compassion. Practicing spirituality brings a sense of perspective, meaning, and purpose to our lives."[1] Having faith in something greater allows us to surrender to the natural unfolding of life and helps us navigate setbacks with resilience. Some people call that greater power God. My husband calls it hiking. Whatever your definition, spirituality helps us to understand the interconnectedness of all beings. We all navigate life with the skills available to us in the present moment. As much as we would like to separate

---
1. Brené Brown, Rising Strong as a Spiritual Practice (Louisville, Colorado: Sounds True, 2017).

ourselves at times, we are all affected by both the pain and joy of others. Spirituality taught me to see the light in others above all else, fostering kindness and a deep understanding that we are all on unique paths, and doing the best we can. When we see the light in others and treat them as if that is all we see, we make an impact and leave a lasting impression on everyone who comes into contact with us.

Spirituality has woven a profound thread that has shaped my journey in ways beyond measure. For most of my life, I saw myself primarily as a successful businesswoman who was also deeply spiritual. However, with age and wisdom, I've realized that I had it backwards. At my core, I am a deeply spiritual woman who possesses strong leadership and business development skills. Embracing this new understanding has been a journey, but it has allowed me to value my spiritual gifts and nature equally with my professional pursuits. It's not about choosing one over the other; it's the synergy between the two that has driven my success. Honoring the balance between them is crucial. By integrating these spiritual gifts into my self-identity, I have achieved a fuller expression and alignment in everything I do. Every task, whether it's a strategy meeting, budgeting, or leading a sales team, can be infused with a spiritual mindset. I have come to realize how essential these practices are for creating career success, becoming a great leader, and finding peace in each moment.

My inner quest for self-mastery is an extremely personal journey, one that I do not share often. My spirituality has been something so personal to me, something that only those who know me well understand. My belief in something greater than myself is the compass that has guided me through times of uncertainty, providing me with the courage to take risks that otherwise might have seemed insurmountable. The impact of spirituality on my life is not a mere footnote; it's the bold headline that narrates my life.

My spiritual journey began when I moved away to Pennsylvania at the age of thirteen. I was so homesick, and in search of comfort anywhere I could find it. I found comfort in food, which created a host of problems. I became so hopeless, depressed, and lonely that I started reading every self-help book I could get my hands on. I studied the Bible, the Quran, shamanism, Buddhism, Hinduism, Christianity, and more. I developed a deeper perspective based on different religions and belief systems and applied that perspective to my daily morning ritual.

Over time, my spirituality became the anchor that allowed me to let go of the outcome, creating space for me to remain present and focused, and trust the process of life's wins and—most importantly—life's failures. How we respond to the experiences surrounding us plays a huge part in our lives. There are so many things we cannot control, but ultimately, if you take extreme ownership of every aspect of your life and forgo living with a victim mentality, you take back your power to truly create the life you want.

True freedom lies in releasing the grip on the reins of control and surrendering to a divine essence that orchestrates a grander plan. This surrender does not denote weakness but embodies a strength found in trusting the intricate process of life. Surrendering also does not mean sitting back and praying something will change. It means a deep commitment to yourself, and trusting you will have the strength, resilience, and courage to withstand life's hardships. We are all inherently worthy—no one person is better than the other. We are each unique and perfect, but we all deserve an equal seat at the table.

In moments where failure and adversity should knock you down and keep you on the ground, spirituality empowers you to rise. It gives you the resilience to face challenges head-on, dust off the setbacks, and continue marching forward. For me, my belief in a divine essence has become a deep well of energy, shaping my outlook on life, the people around me, and my experiences. It gives me the freedom to be seen, vulnerable, and boldly authentic. Perseverance comes from the process of surrendering, and trusting that the Universe has your back no matter what.

Mistakes are never mistakes unless we don't learn from them. Everything in life shows up for our highest good and our greatest learning, and if we do not see it that way, we will constantly be disappointed, discouraged, and eventually, defeated. But know that you already have inside you everything you need to lean into uncertainty, discomfort, challenge, and opportunity. Just like a flower bud already has everything inside of it to bloom to its fullest capacity, so do we. There's no need to prove yourself to others or seek external validation for your worthiness. Spirituality has acted as a guiding force in overcoming every obstacle and struggle I've encountered on my path to achievement. By leaning into our spirituality, we align with the flow of what is greater than ourselves and tap into a powerful energy that transcends individual limitations and connects us to the vast, universal source. For me, spirituality has illuminated the intricate web of connections at the most finite cellular and energetic levels, reminding me that we are all threads in the grand tapestry of the universe.

I love being a student of different religions, not identifying with or labeling myself as a believer of any specific one. Ultimately, the common thread of all religions is love and connectedness. When we adopt this perspective, we realize our individual problems are so minimal in the vast expanse of our universe.

We tend to lose perspective when our problems seem so great. But for me, choosing to believe we are protected by a higher power supporting our every move is like an antidote to anxiety, fear, limiting beliefs, and depression. It's the fuel that propels me forward with confidence and conviction. And it all starts with a deep understanding of ourselves based on an honest look in the mirror, and by releasing ego-protection judgments of ourselves and others.

Criticism comes from a place of insecurity. If you do not consider yourself spiritual, the next time you feel anxious, afraid, angry, depressed, or scared, try thinking about how short your time is here on earth. No problem is ever as big as it seems, because everything is fleeting. Nothing lasts forever—not even the good things—so relax, release the pressure, and enjoy your short time here on Earth.

Imagine yourself at the end of your life, looking back. How do you want to feel? What do you want to think about your life? What kind of things do you want to have accomplished? What do you want people to say about you at your funeral? What kind of impact do you want to have on people's lives? What legacy do you want to leave behind? From that clarity, tailor your present actions, behaviors, energy, thoughts, and beliefs around living out that vision for yourself. If you do this and commit to it, truly, you will have no regrets in your life.

When you live through inspired action, trust that you are living out your best life. In essence, spirituality is not just a belief system; it's a way of living—a philosophy that fosters compassion, resilience, and a profound understanding of our place in the world. Your spirituality can be your guiding light, allowing you to navigate the complexities of life with grace, authenticity, and a deep sense of purpose.

Make Time for Inspiration

Burnout is such a huge problem in Western society. But the way to heal from chronic stress, fatigue, and overwhelm is not more sleep. It is our *souls* that are tired, not our bodies. We need nature. We need adventure. Freedom. Stillness. Truth. And inspiration! We don't need more sleep; we need to wake up and *live*. We need to live like we will not see tomorrow, and love others like it is our last time speaking to them. We need to take the trip, eat that piece of cake, and do pleasurable things in moderation, all while still being

Chapter 2

dedicated, committed, and focused on the life we want for ourselves.

Too often, we see friends, family, colleagues, and others all around us climbing the ladder of success just to be drunk, depressed, and divorced by the time they reach the summit. No matter how committed you are to a goal and how focused you are, if you do not enjoy the journey, what is the point? Take care of your body. Carve out that time just for you every morning, and guard your routines with your life. Rest. Nurture and explore your spirituality, in whatever way that means to you. And above all, make time for *inspiration*. Do these simple things, and you'll already be well on your way to a fulfilled life.

Chapter 3
Find Your Purpose and Passion

The two most important days of your life are the day you were born and the day you find out why.

—Mark Twain

Everything we desire in life gravitates toward our passion and purpose. Passion, rooted in our emotions, represents the embodiment of living in alignment with our values. Purpose is *why* we do what we do, and passion is *what* we do. The question is: What drives you? Those who possess genuine passion have a profound understanding of themselves. They are clear on their values. And they are committed to living authentically.

Purpose serves as the driving force behind our emotions, encapsulating the essence of our "why." It extends beyond personal gain, compelling us to shift our focus from ourselves to others. From a neuroscience perspective, having a clear purpose can reshape our brains, enabling us to block out distractions more effectively. Purpose becomes a powerful ally in times of adversity, fostering perseverance and a burning desire to achieve that outshines the fear of failure. It encourages individuals to sit with the darkness, embracing discomfort, and pushing forward even when the market shifts or discouragement sets in.

Goals are vital to our long-term plans, but sometimes they cause us to lose sight of what's most important. That's why it's so important to understand our purpose. Purpose is what drives us and gives meaning to why we are here. The secret to a fulfilling life is to make sure your goals align with your values, your passion, and your deeper sense of purpose. That's where lasting motivation comes from.

When contemplating your purpose, ask yourself this question: What impact does my work have on others? Understanding the impact of your work and recognizing where you've witnessed its effects can significantly enhance motivation.

As you read this chapter, think about what you truly want. What do you think is stopping you from achieving those goals right now? And who do you need to become to get where you want to go? In my therapy practice, I used to ask my clients, "If you had no fear, what would you do today? What would you do in five years?" I would ask them to think about that question in relation to every area of their lives. When you set fear aside, it's remarkable how much clearer everything suddenly becomes. Without fear, imagine what you could achieve!

If something inspires me, I do it. I follow my passions. But I wasn't always this way. In my twenties, I was easily distracted and constantly compared myself to others. Most of all, I was afraid to be myself. Eventually, I realized I had to overcome that fear. We can't discover our purpose and what we want if we are blinded by fear, and we can't live true to our purpose if we're too busy trying to please others. But when you uncover your true purpose, you tap into an endless source of motivation.

Set aside some time with your journal to think about what you would do today if you removed your fear. What would you change in your life? What would you let go of? What would your life look like, and what would you need to accomplish first in order to get there? Then think about whether your fears are actually true. We waste a lot of time worrying about perceived roadblocks or things that might happen, but a lot of times, those fears aren't even real.

We're also held back by what we think we "should" do rather than what we want. Societal pressures, thoughts and opinions of family and friends, and the disapproval of a spouse can all stop us from living our dream life. We're going to talk about how to let all that go, but first, you need to do some soul-searching. Pursuing your purpose leads to long-term happiness, but you need to figure out exactly what that dream life looks like.

So now that you've taken stock of where you are right now in your life versus where you want to go, let's get to the heart of your purpose and passion, and learn how to prioritize your actions according to what matters most to you. Take some time to ponder these questions:

1. What do you feel called to do in your lifetime?
2. What pursuits light you up?
3. Above all, who do you want to become?

The question "Who do I want to become?" shifts the focus from external achievements to internal growth and transformation. We are always going to be in the process of becoming. The question is, who do you need to become to achieve the goals you set for yourself? As you sit here reading, get honest about who that person is, and who you are now. Create a concrete, clear, actionable commitment to yourself that you will start applying everything you learn in this book to your life every day. Think about how you want to look, how you want to feel, how you want to be perceived, and how you want to make others feel when they think about you. These are all guideposts to help you determine the kind of person you are working to become.

Rather than relying solely on motivation and willpower, this approach emphasizes the development of your character, mindset, and values. True fulfillment comes from aligning your actions with your purpose and passion because the "why" behind your goals gives you an enduring source of motivation.

Willpower is great, but it's only a fraction of the equation for long-term success. It also tends to be fleeting. Long-term happiness comes from the pursuit of purpose and passion rather than fleeting moments of joy. By continually evolving with a growth mindset, you can fully become who you aspire to be. It's an ongoing process of self-discovery and resilience that leads to a more meaningful and fulfilling life.

What Drives Motivation?

Motivational levers can be broadly classified into two categories: *extrinsic* and *intrinsic*, each potent in driving specific outcomes. Extrinsic motivators involve tangible and measurable rewards like bonuses, perks, or recognition (i.e., "employee of the month" awards). These external incentives often reinforce hierarchical structures within organizations, where higher-ups delegate tasks and decide on the rewards.

On the other hand, intrinsic motivators delve into what truly drives behavior, encompassing elements like passion, alignment with values, a sense of belonging, and a clear purpose. Fostering motivation involves developing powerful values, connecting with people, and consistently articulating your purpose.

Discovering and homing in on your core values is a useful exercise in understanding your fundamental motivation. First, identify the values that define you, and then narrow it down to the top five or three most important ones. Self-discipline is pivotal in manifesting your dreams because it helps you act in alignment with long-term goals, regardless of how motivated you feel at any given moment. Extrinsic motivators, like bonuses, may work for measurable outcomes, but they fall short when it comes to engaging your heart and mind. That's where intrinsic motivation is essential.

Extrinsic and intrinsic motivators are different for everyone. You have to discover what these are for you so that you can put them to work. One of the common pitfalls I see organizations make is that they use only one type of motivator for all employees for every company goal. When that motivator fails to produce results, leaders often blame employees for a lack of productivity. Extrinsic motivators don't necessarily fuel intrinsic motivation. Some employees might be inspired by the promise of a bonus, but others might not.

Achieving your goals requires you to change, at least on some level. Lasting behavioral change happens in layers. Your identity drives the outcomes you set and determines who you need to become to reach them. And exactly how you will get there.

Your Purpose and Your Passion

Purpose and passion are equally important in your personal and professional life. Here's a shocking statistic for you: 85 percent of people say they are disengaged at work, according to Gallup's State of the Global Workplace.[2] Given that the average person spends around *90,000 hours at work* over a lifetime, whether you're happy or miserable in your work makes a huge impact on your overall quality of life! I don't know anyone who would willingly choose to be unhappy for 90,000 hours.

---

2. Jim Harter, "Dismal Employee Engagement Is a Sign of Global Mismanagement," Gallup Workplace, accessed November 6, 2024, https://www.gallup.com/workplace/231668/dismal-employee-engagement-sign-global-mismanagement.aspx.

Chapter 3

So the quest for meaning in the work you do isn't merely about personal satisfaction; it's about being more productive, engaged, and successful in every facet of your life. What happens at the office or in your business doesn't just affect your professional life. If you can spend those 90,000 hours engaged in meaningful connections, doing work that helps you express your true self and live out your deeper purpose, imagine the impact on your life overall.

Here's another statistic that underscores the importance of doing purposeful work: According to *Harvard Business Review*, nine out of ten people would willingly trade a percentage of their lifetime earnings for the chance to engage in more meaningful work.[3] A sense of purpose is profoundly important to your well-being and your professional performance.

Finding your purpose is a key element in your journey toward fulfillment. This doesn't mean things will always be easier; sometimes you can find even deeper meaning through trials and setbacks if you can see these challenges as opportunities for learning and gaining a deeper understanding of yourself. It's not about avoiding hardships, but rather embracing them as integral to your pursuit of meaning. Along the way, you learn one of the most important life skills of all: resilience.

Empowering yourself involves recognizing and embracing your unique identity and all the ways you express who you are.

---

3. Shawn Achor et al., "9 Out of 10 People Are Willing to Earn Less Money to Do More-Meaningful Work," Harvard Business Review, November 6, 2018, https://hbr.org/2018/11/9-out-of-10-people-are-willing-to-earn-less-money-to-do-more-meaningful-work.

Authenticity becomes a powerful force, driving your actions in alignment with your personal values and aspirations. Letting go of societal "shoulds" requires releasing self-judgment and refusing to conform to external standards that don't resonate with your true self. This doesn't happen overnight, but gradually, when you align your energy with your goals, your actions become more and more intuitive, inspired, and purpose-driven. When you nurture a mindset of positivity, belief in yourself, and unwavering focus, the path becomes smoother over time.

Homing in on your purpose and passion begins with a deep and honest personal inventory. Start by reflecting on what aspects of your life and work are currently resonating with you. Identify activities or moments that fill you with enthusiasm and energy. Equally important is recognizing what leaves you feeling drained, anxious, or overwhelmed. This duality—what inspires and what causes distress—offers key insights into your true passions and your authentic self.

Once you have a clear picture of what is and isn't working, it's essential to set priorities that align with your newfound understanding. Focus on incorporating more of what excites and motivates you into your daily life and work. Take deliberate steps to minimize or address sources of frustration and anxiety in this process as well. This might mean setting boundaries, delegating tasks, or even reassessing your current commitments to ensure they align with your core values and long-term goals.

Chapter 3

Making a commitment to yourself is a powerful step in translating this self-awareness into meaningful change. Set specific, achievable goals for the next six months that reflect your refined understanding of purpose and passion. Create a plan with actionable steps, and regularly review your progress to stay on track. This commitment not only helps you align your priorities but also reinforces your dedication to living a life that is both fulfilling and true to who you are. By maintaining this focus and making adjustments as needed, you pave the way for a more intentional and passionate life journey.

Prioritize Your Passion

You've clearly identified your purpose and passion. That's great! Now you must learn how to prioritize what deserves your focus. To manifest the achievements you desire, you need to meticulously map out the critical 20 percent of the key activities that produce 80 percent of your desired outcomes. When you're clear on your priorities, you'll always have a compass steering you in the right direction.

One of my favorite books about the philosophy of prioritization is *The ONE Thing* by Gary Keller and Jay Papasan. In the book, they emphasize the distinction between glass balls and rubber balls in our lives. Glass balls symbolize nonnegotiable aspects like family, health, and integrity—those that, if dropped, shatter irreparably. Rubber balls represent priorities we have more flexibility with, like our careers and professional pursuits. Drop a rubber ball occasionally, and it will bounce back. Prioritize glass balls first in your life, and then focus on the rubber balls, dedicating specific time blocks to complete tasks. The idea is to set clear intentions at the start of every day, asking yourself whether you're excited about the day ahead, or dreading it. This gives you powerful insight about whether you're living true to your purpose, and helps you notice when your priorities need to shift. The challenge is to eliminate excuses and *just get it done*—always knowing what can break and what can bend so you don't wind up with a successful career but a broken personal life.

Setting priorities according to your purpose isn't just about time management either. Yes, that's an important skill, but it's also an illusion that implies we have control over an uncontrollable resource. Also, there's a common misconception that time management is purely logical. In reality, it's an emotional endeavor. Every decision we make, including how we decide to spend our time, is deeply influenced by our emotions. We're emotional beings. Despite our awareness of income-producing activities and the plethora of time management advice available, the missing link is the emotional understanding of why we make the choices we do. To fully understand why you grapple with the perpetual struggle to balance productivity with well-being, you have to understand how you feel about how you spend your time and decide what's most important to you.

I would argue that the essence of setting and sticking to your priorities lies in *self*-management, which you *can* control. Setting priorities comprises all the core elements we talked about in the previous chapter: your physical health, emotional/mental well-being, relationships, and spirituality.

It's important to realize, though, that you can't always operate at full capacity. We'll dive deeper into mental and emotional regulation in Chapter 5, but remember that relentless self-management can lead to depletion, burnout, and resentment. The prefrontal cortex, often referred to as the brain's command center, plays a crucial role in controlling how we feel and, more importantly, how we respond to those feelings. Self-regulation is the ability to control emotions and persist when things get tough—key to achieving long-term goals. But It's impossible to balance all the demands and stressors of your life. You can't operate at 100 percent capacity 100 percent of the time. It's just not possible! Always remember that some tasks might not get done. Finding "balance" isn't always possible. The true magic of our efforts often unfolds when we allow ourselves to be temporarily out of balance.

When you find yourself frustrated by a perceived lack of balance or too many tasks left undone, be realistic with yourself. Did you set expectations too high across the board? Maybe you need to temporarily lower the bar. Different phases of life come with distinct stressors and demands. In those moments, short-term habits may take precedence over long-term goals, and that's okay. Balance is dynamic, not static, and a little imbalance here and there, especially when it's intentional, can lead to success in the long run.

Purpose + Prioritization = Supercharged Motivation and Self-Discipline

Prioritization serves as an antidote to the dreaded procrastination. I've devoted all of Chapter 7 to helping you overcome procrastination, but the key thing to understand is that setting priorities according to your purpose amplifies both motivation and self-discipline. Together, that's a powerful driving force! With clear priorities, you're better able to break down complex, big-picture tasks into manageable steps, which helps to mitigate the allure of procrastination. Often, all you need is a little structure to give you direction, boost your motivation, and keep your self-discipline intact. Imagine how much it would decrease your overall stress levels if you didn't have to worry about losing motivation or productivity.

To help you figure out the top priorities that align with your purpose and passion, step outside your daily routine for a minute and imagine your ideal life. Ask yourself questions like "If I could create my life exactly how I wanted it, what would I choose in the areas of health, wealth, and love?" Write down your vision, and revisit this exercise periodically to make sure you're still aligned with your priorities and passion, which may evolve over time. This exercise can highlight the most important factors on your path to a fulfilling existence. After all, you wouldn't want to reach the top of your career only to realize you compromised everything else that nourished your soul, right? Huge success in one area of your life constitutes a profound failure if you have to sacrifice your health, relationships, and financial security to get there.

Chapter 3

We're here to find total fulfillment. Focusing solely on one area yields only a fraction of your potential. Relationships, health, and wealth are interconnected, and directing energy toward all three simultaneously creates a positive feedback loop. As you improve one area of your life, everything else rises too. It's easy to overlook the importance of balance in the pursuit of goals, but the true measure of satisfaction, abundance, and joy emerges when we navigate both the depth and width of our existence. This conscious, daily focus on key aspects in health, wealth, and love creates a life that is not just successful but profoundly fulfilling.

So once you're clear on your purpose, your passion, and your top priorities in all areas of your life, how do you actually put everything in motion? The first step is to craft a schedule that reflects your top priorities. Allocate your time and energy strategically toward activities that align with your big-picture goals in a deliberate effort to design your days with purpose and intention. Your schedule is the visual representation of what truly matters to you—whether that's advancing your career, nurturing your health, or creating more meaningful connections with the people who matter most in your life.

One of the most helpful ways to stay true to your priorities is to find an accountability partner, someone who will be your ally as you pursue your dreams and ambitions. Sharing goals and progress with someone who understands something about why this is so important to you creates both responsibility to your commitments, and a feeling of support, especially when you struggle to stay on course. An accountability partner can give you a much-needed outside perspective, and motivation in the form of a kick in the pants whenever you need it!

You'll also need to remove distractions whenever they appear. These hijackers can take on various forms—everything from incessant phone notifications to unexpected demands on your time, like a last-minute request from a client, or issues that come up at your child's school. Distractions are often unforeseen and persistent, which is why they are a constant threat to your focus. They are inevitable, but simply being prepared ahead of time can go a long way toward lessening their impact. First off, setting clear boundaries on your time and commitments goes a long way. When you're clear on your priorities, it's easier to say "yes" or "no" to unexpected requests. Technology can help you stay on track—and you can always turn off notifications on your phone so you're not tempted to instantly respond to every email or text that comes through.

Yes, prioritizing is an art of balance, but you get to choose which activities derail you, and which ones propel you closer to realizing the fulfilling relationships, feelings of well-being, and professional achievements you long for.

The beauty of setting clear priorities lies in the freedom this gives us. Much like committing fully to a goal, establishing clear priorities is your roadmap for making decisions and taking action. When tasks are organized based on their significance, you'll experience the freedom that comes from knowing exactly how to navigate your responsibilities with purpose and efficiency. It may seem counterintuitive, but by structuring your schedule, you also create more space to relax, rest, and play.

To thrive and succeed, you need to set priorities so that you're never locked in a soul-sucking vortex of ceaseless to-do lists. Think about it this way: we have more resources, knowledge, and technological tools at our disposal than at any other time in history, and yet we work longer hours under more pressure. Why, despite our advancements, has stress reached such unprecedented levels?

If you don't take time to clearly identify the things that light you up and the deeper reasons why you do what you do, and then prioritize your daily activities to lead you to that higher meaning, you will always be weighed down by a pervasive sense of being perpetually behind. That's no way to live. I want you to thrive and succeed. You don't have to choose between achieving your goals and living a fulfilled life full of joy and peace. You can have both!

Speaking of goals, let's go discover how to set goals that speak to your heart.

Chapter 4
Discover Your HEART Goals

Conventional wisdom tells us to adopt SMART goals if we want to reach our aspirations—Specific, Measurable, Achievable, Relevant, and Time-Bound. But there is a better way, a way that brings about deeper meaning and fulfillment, one that looks into the core of our being, intertwining our very identity with our ambitions.

I like to follow the framework of HEART goals:

- H = Honest
- E = Empowering Yourself
- A = All Your People
- R = Recognizing Current Reality
- T = Trajectory

The HEART acronym ensures goals align with who you truly are (not who you pretend to be or the way others perceive you). It empowers your personal passions and guides you to invest in healthy relationships. It takes into consideration all your responsibilities and the reality of your life circumstances, and it adheres to a timely framework for accomplishment. This approach allows you to honor your strengths and unique skills—and ultimately, live every day in alignment with your true power and authenticity.

Instead of focusing on external markers of success the way traditional goal-setting teaches, HEART goals encourage us to explore the person we must become to manifest our deepest desires, acknowledging small wins along the way.

A performance-based goal like "I will lose twenty pounds" becomes the identity-based goal "I am the type of person that never misses a workout." A small win aligning with this identity might involve choosing a morning walk over a run because it felt like what your body needed that day.

The performance-based goal of "I want to increase my income by $50,000 this year," transitions to the identity-based goal "I will always work on my high-priority tasks each day," with a small win of consistently following through on time-blocking throughout the week.

Financial objectives like "I want to get out of debt" transform into "I am the kind of person who never spends more than I make," with small wins like paying off a credit card or initiating a budget with a financial coach.

It's about doing *better*, not less, and with meaningful guidance. HEART goals, whether for the short or long term, propel you closer to your passions and interests, tapping into the full power of your strengths and values. When you do that, you eliminate the need for constant comparison, competition, and compromise. Growing up, and well into my adult life, I was hyperfocused on setting and crushing goals, no matter how exhausted I felt or how little I wanted to keep going. It didn't matter if the pursuit was draining or if my heart wasn't in it anymore; I'd push through. But over time, I realized that I wasn't doing this for myself, or for the right reasons. It was about external measures of success, and I wasn't being kind to myself. Eventually, I started to shift my mindset. I began setting goals that aligned with who I want to become, rooted in my values and self-love, with compassion guiding the way rather than ego or external validation.

HEART goals focus on who you are deep down, promote lasting change, provide meaningful guidance, and follow a holistic approach to success. It's a journey tied to our deeper life's purpose and requires us to embody our goals at the very core of our being. When we set HEART goals, we tap into an internal motivation that's so much more powerful and lasting than anything external. There's a deeper passion and dedication because these goals come from within, reflecting what truly matters to our soul. External factors like recognition or rewards are fleeting and often leave us feeling unfulfilled because they aren't really aligned with who we are. But when it's a HEART goal, nothing can stand in the way because the fuel driving us is passion—not fear, anxiety, or external measurements of "success."

Identity-based HEART goals demand a more profound level of self-awareness. Instead of fixating solely on what we want to accomplish, we shift our focus to who we want to become in the process. For instance, if you aspire to be a disciplined writer, that's an identity-based goal rather than something extrinsic, like aspiring to write a certain number of pages in a specific timeframe. HEART goals align with the principle that sustainable change occurs when our identity resonates with the objectives we set.

When you integrate your identity, internal motivation, and a profound understanding of who you aim to be, HEART goals pave the way for lasting transformation and a more authentic alignment with your deepest desires. HEART goals allow you to let go of the outcomes in favor of focusing on the process and the journey of becoming the best version of yourself. HEART goals also allow you to fit your goals into the life you want to enjoy, living less out of habit and with more intention.

The Purpose and Potency of Setting Goals

Before I walk you through an exercise that will help you set your HEART goals, let's take a closer look at the psychology of goal-setting so that you can understand how fundamental goals are to motivation and personal growth. At the core of human achievement lies the intricate dance between science and psychology, unraveling the purpose and potency of goal-setting. Goals act as beacons guiding us toward our desired future, providing direction and purpose to our actions. They serve as a roadmap, allowing us to envision the possibilities that lie ahead and motivating us to strive for something beyond our current reality.

Chapter 4

Goals serve as the compass that guides our endeavors. The act of setting a goal creates a roadmap to maximize success and minimize failure, paving the way to discovering our greatest potential. Goals offer guideposts along the way so we can manage and measure our progress. If our goals align closely with our higher life's purpose, they become a potent source of motivation and inspiration that help us overcome distraction and procrastination and discover a straighter path to success.

In the realm of psychology, goal-setting acts as a cognitive anchor, channeling our thoughts and energies toward a specific objective. Our minds, prone to wandering about 47 percent of the day, benefit immensely from the structured framework that goals provide.[4] With over 50,000 thoughts traversing our minds daily, a staggering 80 percent of which lean toward the negative, the brain doesn't always operate as an ally.[5] This is precisely why goal-setting becomes a confidant in steering our mental landscape in the right direction.

The Neuroscience of Goal-Setting

The brain plays a key role in setting and achieving goals. The brainstem (particularly the reticular activating system, or RAS) and the prefrontal cortex are key players. Together,

---

4. Alison Escalante, "New Science: Why Our Brains Spend 50% of the Time Mind-Wandering," Forbes, January 28, 2021, https://www.forbes.com/sites/alisonescalante/2021/01/28/new-science-why-our-brains-spend-50-of-the-time-mind-wandering/.

5. Nancy Colier, "Negative Thinking: A Dangerous Addiction," Psychology Today, April 15, 2019, https://www.psychologytoday.com/us/blog/inviting-monkey-tea/201904/negative-thinking-dangerous-addiction.

they orchestrate the symphony of actions needed to propel us toward our aspirations.

The RAS acts as a gatekeeper, sifting a constant influx of sensory information to prioritize what demands immediate attention. Here's what is interesting: the simple act of setting a goal triggers a physiological response, whereby the systolic blood pressure rises, preparing the body for action. Just by setting a goal, we instantly become more ready and zealous to take action.

However, the *size* of the goal matters. If a goal feels overwhelmingly large, it can negatively impact our confidence and even lower systolic blood pressure, acting as a counterforce to action. There's an intricate connection between our mental intentions and our body's responses, which can play against us if we're not fully aware, but we can also use this to our advantage.

The act of writing goals becomes a potent activator of the RAS. As pen meets paper, the brain engages multiple senses, signaling the RAS to prioritize the written goals. The RAS filters information, prioritizing the written goals and bringing aspects related to the set goal and bringing them to the forefront of our conscious awareness. Much like the perceptible surge of motivation when deciding to pursue a certain goal, the RAS responds dynamically to the act of writing down our intentions. So whatever goals you have been thinking in your head, go grab a pen and your notebook and give yourself ten minutes to jot them down with as much detail as you can, and commit to reading those goals daily for one hundred days to begin to establish your keystone habit.

The prefrontal cortex then takes the stage as the architect of task activation. It enables us to focus on present tasks critical for achieving future goals. The time frame associated with a goal becomes significant. If a goal seems too distant, motivation wanes. That's why it's important to break larger goals down into smaller, more manageable steps with milestones that are closer on the horizon.

Visualization is a powerful bridge between intention and action. The prefrontal cortex, influenced by visualization, translates distant goals into immediate, actionable steps. Our imagination allows us to visualize what it will feel like to achieve that goal. Just by picturing the things you want to achieve, you increase your perceived likelihood of achievement. In other words, visualization helps you convince your brain that your goals are feasible.

Athletes understand the transformative power of visualization. Every day, they mentally rehearse those moments of achievement. If you create a clear mental picture of yourself crossing the finishing line of whatever goals you set and imagine it daily, you'll convince your brain that everything you desire is possible. The intricate interplay between the brainstem, RAS, and prefrontal cortex is the mechanism behind goal-setting and achievement. Now that you understand this interplay, you can harness the power of your own brain to transform your intentions into a tangible reality. This is how you propel yourself toward success.

The Anatomy of a Goal

Goal-setting enhances focus, sharpens confidence, and directs your actions with intentionality. By setting and achieving goals, you gain insights into your strengths and capabilities, fostering a positive feedback loop that propels you forward. As you grapple with your mind's ceaseless flow of thoughts, goals are beacons of clarity, grounding you in purpose.

The act of setting goals also empowers you to imagine an ideal future. This is powerful! You will not only be better able to understand your present circumstances, but you'll also allow yourself to establish realistic expectations and the steps you need to take to move forward.

But there's a balance to be struck between setting ambitious goals and avoiding the pitfalls of what I call "goal fatigue." Goal fatigue happens when you've been setting and chasing goals for so long that it leads to exhaustion, making it hard to find the motivation to keep going. After finishing collegiate gymnastics, I was completely burned-out from constantly setting goals around my health and fitness. For many years after, craving the freedom to be carefree, I couldn't even bring myself to set simple goals.

Cognitively, I struggled with wanting to set goals, but deep down—spiritually and subconsciously—I knew I just needed rest. That disconnect created a lot of internal ambivalence, and even some depression, because I didn't understand why I couldn't just push through like I always had. It was frustrating to see myself resisting and doubting my goals when all I really wanted was to just "be" in my life. Eventually, I had to find a new way to balance rest and self-compassion, and still strive for success and achievement without burning out.

Traditional SMART goals do provide a helpful structure to the whole process but can sometimes lead to a compartmentalized view of life because of the focus on easily achievable targets. Instead, HEART goals focus on a broader purpose that balances every part of our lives without becoming overly complicated. HEART goals provide the delicate balance between your abilities, resources, and time.

Goals are not mere aspirations but a nuanced interplay between achievability, believability, and commitment. These three pillars form the bedrock upon which the structure of success is built. Achievability encourages you to stretch your capabilities beyond what you once deemed possible, but not so far that your goals seem out of reach. The human psyche is a delicate landscape, and self-doubt emerges as the number one destroyer of aspirations. The journey toward any goal is often fraught with challenges, and belief in your capacity to surmount obstacles becomes the cornerstone of success. As Henry Ford once said, "Whether you think you can or you think you can't, you're right."

Commitment, the third pillar, is the driving force that propels goals from mere wishes to tangible achievements. It signifies a profound level of determination and grit, setting the stage for an unwavering pursuit of a defined objective. When you commit to yourself, you unleash a transformative energy—an immediate boost of motivation that ignites the journey. This commitment is the pact you make with your aspirations, a binding agreement that fuels your effort over the long term.

Goals Are Catalysts for Change

Goals trigger new behaviors guided by focused action. As soon as you commit to a goal, you also commit to new actions and routines to support that goal. Here's an example. Say you set a HEART goal of becoming a person who puts your health first every day. Suddenly, you have to adopt new habits. You set your alarm an hour earlier each day to make time for your workout and to start packing a healthy lunch. You also hire an assistant to help free up some of your time so you can work shorter hours. Setting a goal flips on the motivational switch. Instead of going through the motions, your daily routines are infused with a new sense of purpose.

There's a beautiful ripple effect here. Setting a goal leads to self-mastery, which creates a surge in confidence—a transformative force that you shouldn't underestimate. Self-confidence propels you to take an honest inventory of your current state versus your desired destination. In turn, this newfound self-assuredness becomes a compass that directs your internal standards, fueling personal growth and development. When you set a HEART goal based on the pillars of achievability, believability, and commitment, you set a ripple effect in motion and fan the flames of motivation. You're not just setting goals, you're sculpting the very contours of your success.

Chapter 4

How to Set Your HEART Goals

Let's go back to the elements of the HEART acronym:

- Honest
- Empowering Yourself
- All Your People
- Recognizing Current Reality
- Trajectory

H = Honest

People often start their self-improvement journey by fixating on the outcomes they want to achieve, such as losing weight, gaining financial success, or completing a significant project. But what you need is an identity change.

This means you may need to alter deep-seated beliefs about yourself, including your worldview; the way you see yourself; self-limiting beliefs; and the judgments, assumptions, and biases you hold about yourself and others. This is why, at the outset of this book, I asked you to take an honest inventory of that reflection you see in the mirror, and then helped you to get to the heart of your true purpose and passion. Identity-based goals are rooted in what you believe about yourself, offering the foundation for lasting behavioral change. Rather than solely focusing on outcomes, identity-based goals prompt you to think about who you need to become in order to achieve those desired results.

Commitment to a goal requires more than just changing actions—it demands a transformation in identity. Becoming the person who has already achieved the goal is vital. For instance, aspiring to lose thirty pounds means identifying as someone who has conquered that challenge. A misalignment in identity might lead to a relapse into old habits, explaining why lottery winners can face financial struggles if they haven't developed the skills and habits to make sound decisions with their money.

The element of honesty also relates to a balance between what's attainable for you, with an element of challenge. A challenging goal can elevate your performance and give you a huge sense of self-satisfaction and pride when you achieve it. Research in goal-setting theory reveals that people adjust their effort levels based on the goal's difficulty. Goals that challenge you not only inspire a winning mindset but also balance effort with reward, driving motivation. But here's a cautionary note: *challenging* should not be confused with *unrealistic*, as the latter can derail your motivation.

E = Empowering Yourself

Setting a goal without clarity is similar to navigating a foggy landscape, leaving you directionless and uninspired. Clarity lights the way. Rather than operating under vague aspirations, ask yourself these questions:

1. What major milestones need to happen for me to achieve my goal?
2. Is this goal something I want, or am I trying to please someone else?
3. What superpowers do I have that will help me along the way?

These questions crystallize the goal and help you understand why it holds transformational power in your personal life, business, and finances. With a clear vision in your mind of who you want to become, you will feel empowered to start the journey, knowing you'll grow a little stronger every day. Goals that align with purpose empower you with the motivational fuel needed for the journey.

Remember, success doesn't merely revolve around achieving specific outcomes, but by embodying a continuous, positive identity that aligns with your vision for personal growth and fulfillment.

A = All Your People

HEART goals center around the impact your work has on others. The Harvard Study of Adult Development, spanning eighty years with eight hundred participants, delved into the intricacies of happiness and unveiled profound insights.[6] The study found that it wasn't the pursuit of wealth or relentless hard work that drives fulfillment. Instead, the true potential for a fulfilling life lies in the enrichment of one's identity through meaningful and sustaining relationships. The study emphasizes the importance of social connections, which are paramount to enduring mental and emotional well-being. Relationships have a transformative impact on our lives. Genuine happiness stems from meaningful human connections.

---

6. Pierre Buttin, "What the Longest Study on Human Happiness Found Is the Key to a Good Life," Atlantic, January 19, 2023, https://www.theatlantic.com/ideas/archive/2023/01/harvard-happiness-study-relationships/672753/.

It's noteworthy that a majority of people would willingly exchange years from their lives for more meaningful work and deeper connections, highlighting the profound importance of these motives in driving motivation and performance. When you set goals that are driven by the greater purpose of connection, social bonds, and being part of something larger, you will ultimately have a powerful motivating force on your side.

R = Recognizing Current Reality

The next phase spans changing habits and systems, and implementing new routines or practices that align with the desired identity. When we're setting goals, it's essential to take responsibility for our current reality so that we can get a clear picture of where we actually are versus where we want to be. This means being honest with ourselves about our strengths, weaknesses, resources, and limitations. By acknowledging our true starting point, we can better define what needs to change or improve. From there, we can conduct a gap analysis, identifying the specific steps, skills, or shifts required to bridge that gap between our current state and our desired outcome. This approach creates a realistic and actionable path to achieving our goals. Habits are the building blocks at this level, influencing daily actions and behaviors.

These identity-based habits and systems naturally lead to changing outcomes—tangible results like weight loss, financial gain, winning a competition, or completing a book. The key lies in recognizing that true transformation starts with altering who we are in relation to what we want, fostering a holistic and sustainable approach to personal growth. And remember, a growth mindset—a fundamental element—involves finding meaning in trials and setbacks. This mindset positions challenges as opportunities for learning and growth rather than insurmountable obstacles. Empowering oneself and embracing unique expression involve letting go of societal expectations, self-judgments, and external standards.

T = Trajectory

Trajectory plays a huge role in setting goals because it's all about the long-term direction, not just the individual steps along the way. It's important to stay focused on the bigger picture—what kind of growth, happiness, and abundance we want in our lives. Even when we're hitting milestones, if the overall path isn't aligned with our values and vision, we can end up feeling unfulfilled. That's why it's crucial to check in with ourselves and make adjustments when we start to drift off course, ensuring we're staying true to our long-term potential.

I experienced this firsthand when I took certain job positions that looked great on paper. Deep down, I knew they didn't align with the future I envisioned for myself. Despite what others thought and how much sense those roles made from the outside, I eventually followed my intuition. I could see that the trajectory wasn't leading me toward the life or person I wanted to be. It wasn't about the paycheck or the title; it was about living my best life, one that felt authentic to me. So, even though it was a tough decision, I trusted that vision and made changes, and it ultimately led me toward a path that felt much more aligned with who I truly am.

The crux of achieving lasting success lies not in laziness or a lack of effort but rather in the art of setting goals correctly. It's a common misconception that goals fail due to insufficient hard work, when in reality, the key lies in aligning them with our identity. The pathway to sustainable change is paved through identity-based habits—a recognition that we become who we believe ourselves to be.

Identity-based goals, rooted in our values and the person we aim to become, grant a sense of effortlessness to our actions. This alignment resonates across various aspects of life. Our identity is a reservoir of strength, a core aspect of our character that shapes how we perceive ourselves in the world, and it is malleable, subject to change over time. The essence lies in the understanding that in life, we don't receive what we merely want; we receive what we truly are.

Chapter 5
Mental and Emotional Regulation

One of the reasons why I love the challenge of running a marathon is that it's me against myself. Everyone in the race has the same opportunity to succeed. Whether I finish the race or give up halfway through my training is entirely up to me.

When I decided to train for my first marathon in 2020, I was unable to run three miles without stopping. As the training schedule got more challenging and I had to run more miles each day, my motivation went down. Running sixteen miles in the rain at 5:00 a.m. wasn't exactly inspiring! This is where my habits of self-discipline prevailed because it was no longer about how motivated I felt in each moment but about a deep commitment to myself that got me through those long morning runs.

Just like training for a marathon, writing this book has been a journey of commitment, self-discipline, and discovery. As I peeked back at my journey's montage, I realized the difference between those who accomplish what they set out to do and those who do not lay in the two secret ingredients that have silently shaped my entire life. Enter the dynamic duo: focus and self-discipline.

Self-Discipline: The Architect of Success

Self-discipline is the architect of success, the special ingredient that turns dreams into reality. Self-discipline transcends the ebb and flow of motivation. The journey toward personal betterment isn't solely reliant on your fleeting feelings but a profound commitment to your growth. Far from being punitive, self-discipline is a compassionate self-acknowledgement of areas where we fall short of our fullest potential. Self-discipline is not a rigid set of rules. Think of it as a dance between control and freedom. It's found in surrendering to the habits that you know will get you closer to what you desire. It is the total belief that by focusing day in and day out on what you want your life to look and FEEL like—with the power of letting go and surrendering to the process of time—consistency and total commitment will get you over the finish line.

Self-discipline is about resisting the inclination to succumb to adversity or sidestep necessary tasks you don't want to do. We're all human—we all struggle with these temptations. But results are born not from fixating on the end goal; they're born from concentrating on the small, incremental habits and behaviors that lead to long-term success. Self-discipline will get you where you want to go, and it requires an ability to forgo short-term satisfaction for long-term gratification. If your goal is to lose thirty pounds, but you struggle to commit to the actions and habits necessary to achieve that goal, you will never lose the weight.

Trusting yourself to make decisions and follow through, even when you face inner resistance or a drop in motivation, gives you a profound boost in confidence. Self-trust is transformative, transcending the grip of limiting beliefs and paving the way for personal growth. Confidence is often born out of the courage to act in alignment with your decisions, which in turn becomes a powerful force in shaping your self-perception and interactions with the world. When you push through inner resistance and pursue your goals despite the discomfort, you develop a sense of self-discipline that is instrumental in achieving lasting success. This self-discipline is not about motivation; it's about embracing the uncomfortable and persevering despite how you feel. You see, motivation is fleeting, and we as humans all struggle with a lack of motivation at times. The good news is that you are fully in control of your conscious decision to craft a roadmap toward personal excellence and pave the way for a more purposeful existence.

Self-discipline comes down to the ability to regulate your emotions and mindset. Mental and emotional self-regulation kicks in during those times when you just don't feel like doing what you know you need to do to accomplish your goals. This is true for anything you want to achieve in life, whether it's building your sales business, writing a book, saving money to go on a dream trip, or running a marathon. All of those things require self-discipline because the pursuit of those things outweigh momentary motivation. It requires fortitude, focus, and a commitment that prevails over fleeting emotions and limiting self-talk that keep you held back from what you truly want to accomplish.

The ability to regulate and control your emotions becomes a linchpin for various aspects of your life influencing your health, self-confidence, relationships, and how you navigate setbacks. Let's get down to the nitty-gritty of learning how to master the most important life skill of all.

The Ultimate Superpower

The ability to regulate your thoughts and emotions so they align with how you *want* to think and feel—and take action accordingly—is the ultimate superpower.

Your life's aspirations hinge on mastering your emotions and your mindset. Without this ability, everything else crumbles. But mental and emotional regulation skills are also the hardest personal development skills to achieve. You have to commit every day to developing your self-awareness and self-control. I'm sure you've heard some variation of the Epictetus saying: "It's not what happens to you, but how you respond that makes the difference." Life will inevitably throw challenges your way, and you have to be able to respond in a way that aligns with your beliefs, goals, and intentions.

Mastering your mindset and emotional regulation system can be extremely difficult, but the reward is that this skill has the potential to change your life. Whether you want to simply feel more confident, be a better leader, stop being afraid to pick up the phone and generate sales, run a marathon, or simply feel more at peace throughout your day, mental and emotional regulation is essential. As a real estate broker, I work with hundreds of clients and co-brokers who have different personalities and varying levels of emotional intelligence, so I have to be able to assess each situation and respond accordingly—not react. This skill has allowed me to connect with and work with just about anyone.

Emotional regulation, similar to keeping emotions between the guardrails, is closely tied to how you show up in various aspects of your life. Acting according to your thoughts, rather than succumbing to fleeting feelings, reinforces a sense of control over your responses and actions. This enables you to overcome emotional hurdles and stay focused on your objectives, which in turn builds resilience in the face of adversity.

No amount of coaching, reading books, going to the gym, participating in memberships, or watching motivational YouTube videos can yield your desired outcome if your internal fortitude to persevere is lacking. You must learn how to follow through and handle difficult situations with clarity and control.

In essence, when you trust yourself to navigate decisions with determination and exercise self-discipline, you create a positive feedback loop that reinforces your ability to regulate your emotions and confront challenges. This, in turn, contributes not only to personal success but also to a more balanced and resilient approach to life's complexities. Your journey of making decisions and following through becomes a testament to your inner strength and capacity for growth.

The Neuroscience of Emotion and Behavior

In the realm of behavioral psychology and neuroscience, emotional intelligence is a key focus. Growing scientific evidence underlines the significance of emotional intelligence (EQ) over traditional intelligence (IQ) in determining happiness and success. EQ surmounted the understanding and management of emotions, incorporating facets like emotional awareness, self-regulation, social skills, empathy, and motivation. Numerous studies demonstrate that a high level of emotional intelligence is strongly linked to enhanced career success and overall well-being. Recognizing the impact of EQ on our success exemplifies the importance of cultivating these skills.

As a former cognitive behavioral therapist (CBT) with a passion for neuroscience and human behavior, I've explored the intricacies of how emotional intelligence contributes to overall mental health. Before transitioning into real estate sales, my work at Maine Medical Center involved assisting patients dealing with depression, anxiety, substance abuse issues, and trauma. As a result, they had little control over what and how they thought. My primary emphasis was on helping them comprehend faulty thought patterns and providing tools to identify and alter unhelpful behavioral tendencies.

Over time, with practice and awareness, they were able to notice, reframe, and replace unhelpful thought patterns and reactions with healthier, more rational responses.

The essence of emotional intelligence lies in understanding the why and how behind our behavior. By approaching it with curiosity rather than judgment, we create a conducive environment for personal growth and positive change. Shame, often associated with judgment, proves counterproductive to fostering meaningful transformation. Acknowledging the role of emotional intelligence allows individuals to engage in self-reflection with an open mind, paving the way for constructive adjustments.

The understanding gained from the intersection of emotional intelligence, neuroscience, and behavioral therapy points out the profound impact it can have on personal development. The ability to navigate emotions, build strong social connections, and develop motivation not only contributes to career success but also enhances overall happiness and fulfillment in life. Embracing the principles of emotional intelligence offers a holistic approach to understanding and improving ourselves, creating a foundation for sustained well-being and success.

Emotions are core to our everyday behavior and play a central role in our self-discipline. Our brain, likened to a low-powered computer, operates on a fundamental principle of preserving energy and avoiding pain or discomfort. Procrastination often stems from an emotional regulation issue—a mechanism to avoid tasks that evoke uncomfortable emotions. When we give in to procrastination or fail to uphold personal commitments, we subtly erode our self-confidence and self-trust. This erosion creates a reservoir of low self-esteem, making it increasingly challenging to follow through on promises.

Each time we neglect our commitments, whether it's hitting the snooze button on a morning workout or postponing a task, we send a message to our subconscious that we cannot be relied upon. Trust in oneself is a significant component of self-discipline, relying on the assurance that once we make a decision, we will follow through. It's important to remember that perfection is an unattainable goal. Embarking on a journey of self-discipline involves pinpointing and understanding our thought patterns that contribute to unhelpful behavioral cycles. Many of these patterns may operate beneath our conscious awareness, making it crucial to examine the intricacies of our thoughts.

Individuals who lack emotional regulation skills often find themselves susceptible to being easily distracted and pulled off track, especially in this day and age of overstimulation and constant bombardment by external stimulation. These people may exhibit significant reactions to events, struggle with impulse control, and find it challenging to cope with unexpected hurdles. The absence of effective emotional regulation can lead to intense mood swings, creating a roller coaster of emotions that impact both personal and professional aspects of life.

The challenges associated with poor emotional regulation can manifest in various ways, from difficulty focusing on tasks due to constant distractions, to an inability to handle unexpected obstacles. In professional settings, these individuals may find it challenging to maintain composure and respond appropriately in high-pressure situations. This can affect decision-making, teamwork, and overall job performance. In personal relationships, the lack of emotional regulation skills can lead to strained interactions. The intensity of emotional reactions may create an environment of unpredictability, making it difficult for others to understand and connect with the individual. This, in turn, can strain relationships and hinder effective communication.

Furthermore, the struggle with impulse control can have a significant impact on one's ability to follow through on personal commitments. The impulsive nature may lead to decisions made in the heat of the moment, without careful consideration of consequences. This can result in a pattern of unfulfilled commitments, causing frustration for both the individual and those around them. Addressing and improving emotional regulation skills becomes crucial for mitigating these challenges. Developing the ability to manage and express emotions constructively not only enhances personal well-being but also positively influences the dynamics of professional and personal relationships. It enables individuals to navigate life's challenges more effectively, fostering resilience and promoting a more stable and fulfilling existence.

Understanding human behavior in the context of self-discipline requires an exploration into the evolution of our brains over centuries. The brain has adapted to changing conditions, providing us with the ability not only to survive but also to collaborate, communicate, and problem-solve. However, the mechanisms to regulate emotions did not always exist. In moments of difficulty, feelings and emotions take the wheel, relegating cognition and logical problem-solving to the background. Intense emotions can even cause our brain to go "offline," making conscious decision-making impossible.

At the core of our brain, the brainstem houses the "fight, flight, or freeze" center. In response to discomfort, we instinctively move toward it, move away from it, or fight against it. Moving toward discomfort may involve people-pleasing or overcommitting. Moving away from it might manifest as hiding or self-sabotage. And fighting against discomfort may lead to using shame or aggression as coping mechanisms. The challenge lies in looking at these responses without judgment. Developing self-discipline involves getting comfortable with being uncomfortable, allowing us to maintain our integrity even when faced with challenging situations.

This journey toward self-discipline is intertwined with understanding, managing, and embracing the emotions that guide our everyday behavior. Take a moment to self-reflect on the primary emotions that drive your behaviors throughout the day. Are they moving you closer to your goals? Which emotion is in the driver seat of your life most days? Take some time to reflect, and identify areas where you may want to be more mindful of which primary emotion drives your thoughts and behaviors.

Chapter 5

Emotions Serve a Purpose

It's essential to acknowledge that all emotions serve a purpose, and none are inherently bad. Embracing a healthy approach to emotional expression entails finding a balance between overwhelming emotions (where we lose all sense of control) and experiencing no emotions at all (leading to apathy and complacency). The key lies in emotional *regulation* rather than *repression*. The goal is not to sweep emotions under the rug but to understand and manage them effectively.

Regulating emotions requires acknowledging the presence of emotions, understanding their origins, and finding constructive ways to express and process them. Repression, on the other hand, involves pushing emotions aside without addressing their root causes, leading to a buildup of unresolved feelings.

When I was practicing as a clinician, I worked with adolescents and teens with behavioral and intellectual disabilities, often providing family support and therapy as well. One main focus was to help the parents and guardians understand how to address behavioral issues in a way that was productive and didn't further disrupt the child or the family dynamic. When children or adolescents experience big emotions, those who act as their support system must learn to help them regulate their emotions by asking clarifying questions and acknowledging their emotions and feelings from a loving and, most importantly, neutral place.

Whether you are a parent helping your child navigate intense emotions, or you are trying to develop these skills yourself, it's vital to promote an awareness of your emotional landscape. You need to learn to recognize the patterns of behavior triggered by specific emotions and understand how these patterns impact your ability to fulfill your commitments. By approaching emotions with curiosity rather than judgment, you create a space for growth and transformation. The journey toward self-discipline encompasses not just the act of making commitments but also the development of emotional intelligence and regulation, ensuring a holistic approach to personal development.

How to Master Mental and Emotional Regulation

Regulating emotions daily involves cultivating mindfulness and awareness in your everyday activities. Start by paying attention to routine tasks such as driving, eating, washing dishes, or even petting your dog. Approach these activities with a sense of presence, just noticing and observing, congruent to watching clouds pass by. Externalizing your focus decreases the power of overwhelming emotions, allowing you to step back and gain perspective.

A crucial aspect of emotional regulation is recognizing that you are not defined by your emotions; they are a part of you. It helps to simply name your emotions as you feel them. By identifying and naming the emotion, you begin the process of observation, description, and acceptance. When you externalize your emotions and simply acknowledge them without judgment, this can liberate you. This act alone allows you to stop trying to avoid or run away from your emotions and instead shift your attention to a positive new thought.

It's important to realize that just because you feel an emotion, it doesn't mean you have to take immediate action. It's okay to sit with emotions for a while. Acting impulsively can often intensify and prolong the emotion. Impulses—those automatic subconscious reactions—frequently go unnoticed, but they often reflect your unmet needs. This is key. For instance, reaching for an extra slice of cake might signify tiredness or discomfort. Every time you give in to an impulse, you reinforce that behavior. It's crucial to question and understand your underlying motivations before you act on impulse. This process of mindfulness and thoughtful consideration can significantly contribute to healthier emotional regulation in your daily life.

Let's look at the key pillars of emotional regulation:

1. **Decrease Intensity**

    Simply acknowledge and observe your emotions, giving them space. The goal is regulation, not repression. It's crucial not to sweep emotions under the rug. Emotions are important, but recognize that as humans, we can observe and manage them without letting them control our actions. Also, feeling an emotion doesn't mean *becoming* that emotion. For instance, one can feel annoyance, anger, or fear and simply notice these emotions without internalizing them or taking action on them.

2. **Shift Attention Away from Unhelpful Thoughts**

   Practice taking the opposite action to shift attention away from the unhelpful thought. For example, when you're seventeen miles into a run and start to think about exhaustion, consciously focus on perseverance instead of giving in to the desire to stop.

3. **Inhibit Acting on Impulse**

   Recognize and feel impulses without *becoming* them. Impulses are automatic subconscious reactions, and self-discipline involves the willingness to forgo short-term gratification for long-term satisfaction and gain. Every time you give in to an impulse, you reinforce that behavior. Challenge yourself by asking how you'll feel in the short and long term when faced with an impulse. Consider whether the impulse aligns with your goals. For instance, when the impulse is to skip a morning run while training for a marathon, ask if it brings you closer to your goal.

4. **Breathe and Practice Mindfulness**

   Practice deep breathing and mindfulness techniques. Pay attention to daily tasks and activities, bringing awareness to even the most mundane, like washing dishes or brushing your teeth. Mindfulness enhances your awareness of the present moment, which fosters a sense of control over your emotions and impulses.

Chapter 5

Thoughts, Emotions, Actions—and Shitty First Drafts (SFD)

Emotions, at their core, consist of three interconnected components:

1. Our thoughts, which dictate how we experience the emotion
2. Our feelings, which represent the bodily sensations associated with these emotions
3. Our behaviors, which encapsulate our reactions to the feelings we experience

The relationship between thoughts, emotions, and actions is a dynamic interplay that significantly shapes our responses to various situations. In this intricate process, thoughts serve as the initial catalyst, setting the stage for the emotional response. This pattern is often referred to as the "action tendency," emphasizing the inclination or tendency to act in a certain way based on our emotions. However, the keyword here is "tendency." Feeling a certain way does not mandate a specific action. It's crucial to recognize that we possess the agency to act differently from our initial emotional inclination.

For instance, we can experience anger but choose to respond calmly, feel fear yet act courageously, or feel discouraged but persist. This capacity to act counter to our initial emotional tendency highlights the flexibility inherent in our emotional responses. It accentuates the power of our conscious decision-making and the ability to override automatic reactions.

The stories we tell ourselves in response to our emotions play a key role in shaping our behaviors. Whenever we face a situation that triggers an emotional response, we instantly create a story around it. I often refer to that initial narrative as the "shitty first draft," a term I've borrowed from author Anne Lamott's book *Bird by Bird*, which talks about how the first draft of any writing project is inherently bad, and that's okay. But when it comes to our emotions, that initial "badly written" story can trigger a negative feedback loop that reinforces our limiting beliefs and influences subsequent actions. When we recognize that our first story draft is always going to be shitty and need revision, we learn to intervene consciously, challenging and reshaping the stories we tell ourselves before we act on them. By rewriting these narratives, we gain agency over our emotional responses—fostering resilience, adaptability, and the ability to constructively navigate the complexities of our inner world.

Here are two exercises to help you rewrite your "shitty first drafts" into more powerful stories.

Exercise 1

1. Pick a recent event that resulted in an undesirable outcome.

    Example: You took your frustrations out on your spouse after a challenging day at work.

2. Contemplate your initial thoughts and beliefs (your SFD), and identify your underlying behaviors that contributed to your reaction.

Example Thought: I'm overwhelmed, unappreciated, or unsupported.

Belief: I must handle everything on my own; no one understands my struggles.

Emotion Resulting from SFD: Feeling overwhelmed and unappreciated, leading to frustration and resentment.

3. Identify the action you took as a result of your emotion.

    Example: "I expressed dissatisfaction and irritation; I spoke in a way that hurt my spouse and provoked an argument. This was an unhealthy coping mechanism arising from my belief that nobody understands the stress I am feeling."

4. Create an alternative approach for emotional regulation.

    Identify the SFD and challenge it. Instead of assuming no one understands, communicate your feelings and seek support. Choose a healthier coping mechanism, such as expressing your feelings without projecting them onto others, or taking a moment for self-reflection before you say anything or react.

This exercise illustrates how thoughts and beliefs contribute to emotions and subsequent actions. By understanding and challenging your underlying beliefs, you can choose more constructive actions that promote emotional well-being and healthier relationships.

Exercise 2

High emotional regulation skills give you a profound awareness of your initial, often negative, thought patterns—your SFDs. Instead of succumbing to automatic thought loops, you develop the ability to consciously reframe and replace these initial narratives. This exercise will help you develop a proactive and intentional approach to shaping your thoughts and subsequent emotions. By acknowledging and challenging your initial stories, you can redirect your thought processes toward more constructive and positive narratives. This intentional reframing not only disrupts detrimental automatic loops but also empowers you to navigate your emotional landscapes with resilience and purpose, fostering a more positive and adaptive mindset.

This exercise shows you how to leverage visualization, understand your desired feelings, and enhance supportive thoughts to drive the outcomes you seek.

1. **Get clear on your desired outcome:**

    Visualization is a powerful tool to gain clarity on your desired outcome. Envision the specific scenario or situation in which you want to achieve a positive outcome. Define the end goal clearly, considering both short-term and long-term objectives.

2. **Identify the desired feeling to drive action:**

    Explore the emotions associated with the desired outcome, and consider how you need to feel to drive the desired action. For example, if your goal is to excel in a presentation, the desired feelings might include confidence, enthusiasm, and focus.

3. **Understand the thoughts that support your desired feeling:**

   Pinpoint thoughts that support the desired feelings and subsequent actions. Challenge any negative or counterproductive thoughts that may hinder the desired emotional state, and cultivate positive affirmations or thoughts that align with the emotions necessary for the desired outcome. For instance, if confidence is essential, thoughts could include past successes, skills, or positive feedback.

4. **Use visualization Techniques:**

   Practice visualization exercises regularly. Close your eyes and vividly imagine yourself in the desired scenario, experiencing the positive emotions associated with success. Visualization enhances mental rehearsal, reinforcing the connection between thoughts, feelings, and actions.

5. **Develop an intentional mindset:**

   Develop an intentional mindset by consciously choosing thoughts that align with the desired outcome. Be aware of any self-limiting beliefs, and actively replace them with empowering thoughts. Consider creating a mental mantra or phrase that encapsulates the positive mindset required. For example, when I get up to present in front of a large audience, I visualize myself pushing energy through my feet into the ground to center and neutralize any nervousness, and visualize my audience feeling motivated, inspired, and empowered after my speech.

6. **Reinforce a positive feedback loop:**

   Recognize the cyclical nature of thoughts, feelings, and actions. As positive thoughts drive desired emotions and actions, acknowledge and celebrate small victories. This positive feedback loop reinforces the connection between intentional thoughts and successful outcomes, creating a self-perpetuating cycle of success.

Healthy emotional expression operates within the delicate balance between overwhelming emotions—where you risk losing all sense of control—and the absence of emotions, which can lead to complacency. The secret weapon in your arsenal is the ability to detach from outcomes, allowing you to stay present and retain perspective. When you let go of attachments, you can then embrace the freedom that comes with letting them go.

Embracing the art of keeping your thoughts, feelings, and emotions in check despite how you feel in each moment requires daily commitment to live the life of your dreams. In the next chapters, you'll learn how to prioritize those commitments, create a schedule to help you stick to them, and use techniques like time-blocking to make sure you always follow through. You're also going to learn how to adopt healthy habits (and let bad habits go) that cultivate success in the long run.

Ultimately, self-discipline (and the mental and emotional regulation that underpins that self-discipline) is about taking each day as it comes, trusting that your consistent dedication and focus to the daily grind will naturally propel you toward your ultimate goals. To refine this trait, heightened self-awareness is indispensable. The skill, similar to toning a muscle at the gym, is universally accessible. It calls for consistent, deliberate practice—a gradual process of molding yourself into someone capable of steering your course independent of leading emotions. Your journey of self-discipline unfolds through steady intentional effort over time, and becomes a unique part of your identity.

Wisdom lies in the knowledge that if you overestimate short-term gains and underestimate the cumulative impact of sustained effort over time, this can lead to misguided expectations and unrealistic goals. Mental and emotional regulation requires daily commitment, but your hard work will pay off in spades. It's a holistic transformation that emanates from within. Work to improve every day, and you'll be well on your way to a life of joy, happiness, and fulfillment.

Chapter 6
Blasting through Ambivalence

Ambivalence has played a significant role in various aspects of my life, causing both suffering and complacency. One poignant example is my journey to regain health and fitness after my gymnastics career ended. Initially, I approached it with an extreme, all-or-nothing mindset, embracing rigorous regimens and making considerable sacrifices. But this only caused me to rebel against myself and fall into a cycle of frustration, disappointment, and lack of follow-through. For many years, I could not understand why I was unable to force myself into submission to follow strict self-imposed rules and regimen, much like I had done my entire life as a competitive gymnast. What I later came to realize is that my internal world was in complete conflict. I hit goal fatigue, where complacency set in and progress stalled. I found myself stuck.

To get back on track and develop a new, sustainable approach to my health, I had to first get to the bottom of my internal resistance. Where was it coming from? I knew it couldn't be from simply pushing myself too hard. I needed to fundamentally shift my approach and figure out a way to set my fitness goals from a place of purpose. I needed to gain an understanding of how my fitness played into my overall fulfillment. I began to see that my internal resistance stemmed from unresolved conflict and burnout. My spirit wanted to rest, but my ego was still forging forward with the same expectations and beliefs around goal-setting and achievement that I'd had as a collegiate gymnast.

I realized I was too focused on perfection, when I needed to focus on progress instead. This shift in mindset allowed me to navigate my internal conflicts and create a space where I could move forward without the paralyzing pressure of perfection. I had to learn to find joy in the process of making choices that felt good for my body and my mind. I needed to act from a place of passion rather than pressure.

Rethinking my approach extended beyond health and fitness, influencing how I tackled various goals in my career as well. Embracing the concept of progress over perfection became a guiding principle, alleviating the burden of ambivalence. This transformation illuminated the path toward self-mastery, showing that acknowledging imperfections and valuing progress are powerful tools in overcoming internal conflicts and achieving sustainable growth.

Addressing internal ambivalence is integral to your journey toward a fulfilling life. It has a dramatic impact on your alignment and, subsequently, your ability to attain self-mastery. Ambivalence is the gray area of wanting two things equally without clarity about your next step. It doesn't mean you don't care; it means you have such mixed feelings about a particular thing, that you can't choose or move forward. Ambivalence generates stress and internal resistance, often leading to a desire to escape—or worse, succumb to apathy and complacency. I see this all too often with people who have all of the skills, knowledge, and talent in the world but can't seem to get out of their own way. They have fallen victim to the cycle of complacency and action paralysis.

Ambivalence arises when our thoughts, feelings, and actions are not in alignment, creating a complex inner landscape of resistance and confusion. Ambivalence often rears its head when we've experienced repeated failures in making significant life changes, be it in our lifestyle or career. For me, my perceived failure to achieve my Olympic dream as a gymnast created so much fear later on that I overcompensated by pushing myself too hard for perfection. In my desire for success, I remembered what it took to achieve my previous goals, and it made me afraid to go back down that path. Although I felt a deep desire for my goals, I also felt fear, which created ambivalence.

In moments of self-doubt and fear, this collision often occurs subconsciously, manifesting as internal resistance. This resistance becomes a formidable barrier, eroding self-confidence and hindering our ability to commit wholeheartedly to change. The clash between the desire for transformation and the apprehension rooted in fear can generate a sense of being stuck in limbo, torn between two opposing forces. Navigating this ambivalence demands a deep introspection to unearth the underlying fears and doubts, fostering a conscious awareness that allows you to address and overcome your internal conflict so that you can continue your journey toward change. In my case, I had to remember that I wasn't trying to train for the Olympics anymore—I just wanted to get my health and fitness back on track!

When internal conflicts go unresolved, even those seemingly inconsequential, they create a misalignment that hinders progress in a profound way. Internal conflict is often intricate in nature and shows up everywhere in our lives. Someone's desire to grow a sales team, for example, may be clouded by fear of failure. An entrepreneur who aspires to generate more business may feel conflicted because they have concerns about sacrificing family time to grow their business. The ambition to become healthy might be at odds with potential sacrifices, like waking up earlier or giving up free time or time with family in order to devote more time to exercise.

The toll of ambivalence is far-reaching. The emotional conflict breeds not only complacency but also procrastination, causing a push-and-pull dynamic that undermines self-esteem, motivation, self-trust, and the ability to make decisions. The relentless struggle of ambivalence can leave you feeling stuck, unable to make a change despite a strong desire to transform. The more you suppress your conflicting emotions, the more intense your internal struggle. The result? An endless cycle of stagnation and frustration.

Chapter 6

Self-discipline requires us to buy into our goals, 100 percent. It requires a deep commitment to ourselves that leaves no room for internal conflict. When we wholeheartedly desire something, without a shred of ambivalence, we can approach it with unwavering dedication, clarity, and confidence. The absence of conflicting emotions allows us to formulate a plan of attack and execute it almost effortlessly. This level of commitment enables us to dive headfirst into our goals, free from the doubts sown by ambivalence.

The struggle becomes even more apparent when we recognize that the change we seek is hindered by the comfort and security of the familiar, even when it holds us back. We might understand the need for a lifestyle shift, a career move, or new habits, yet find comfort in the familiarity of our current situation. It's the fear of the unknown—the discomfort of stepping out of our comfort zone—that fuels ambivalence. For instance, your desire to create structure by scheduling your time might be overshadowed by the fear of releasing control.

The good news is that there's a solution! First, you must unravel these conflicting sentiments so that you can address them head-on and find solutions. Once you fully understand why you are torn between two opposing goals, you can find a way to prioritize your actions and break free from stagnation so you can achieve a sense of internal harmony.

Remember, success is hard work! It requires continual learning, studying, perseverance, sacrifice—and most of all, a love for what you're doing. But ambivalence depletes your energy. That's why it's so important to align your energy to address the internal ambivalence that keeps you from moving in the direction of your desires. Having positive and negative feelings about change is normal. How we identify and address those feelings, in ourselves and in those we serve, can positively impact the change process.

At the heart of it, we're talking about human freedom.

We all strive to be the primary movers in our own lives. We tend to rebel—either openly or in secret—against various forms of control, even when these forms of control are meant to help us. We're designed to resist coercion. By addressing ambivalence, you will feel empowered to make decisions for change based on all the information—the full and truthful picture, not just the positive side. Being ambivalent is hard emotional work, so people often resolve it by not thinking about one side. This solution is inadequate and does not lead to an honest, fulfilling life. Being able to identify and face your ambivalence is an integral skill that will serve you well in your own thoughts about change.

Contemplating Change

Ambivalence is a natural aspect of the prolonged process of change, often surfacing during the second stage of change: the **contemplation stage**. Unlike the precontemplation stage of change, where we have no awareness of the negative impact of our behavior, the contemplation stage of change occurs when we first acknowledge a behavior we want to modify because we understand its detrimental impact, yet we find ourselves hesitant or trapped in uncertainty about how to initiate change. The journey from the familiar to the unfamiliar requires a leap of faith, as the consequences of life-altering decisions are inherently unpredictable. Unless a situation is dire, prompting immediate action for physical, emotional, or psychological safety, there may not be an urgent need to act.

Change proves challenging because we seek plausible rationalizations to avoid it, clinging to familiar patterns even when we are aware that our current state no longer serves us. The key lies in resisting the urge to rationalize why we should maintain the status quo. Instead, we have to summon the courage to look inward and shed light on the ambivalence within. Understanding that change is a gradual evolution rather than an immediate demand can alleviate the pressure, encouraging a more thoughtful and deliberate approach to transformative endeavors.

Accepting and recognizing where you currently stand in the process is essential. This is when you start to view ambivalence as a positive sign rather than a hindrance—a signal that introspection has begun. You no longer comfortably embrace the status quo. It's crucial to honestly assess whether you're ready for the change, or if redirecting energy toward other pursuits might be more beneficial.

Initiating change demands a commitment to self-discipline and decisive action rather than mere contemplation. If your dreams have lingered in the realm of conversation without tangible progress, it's essential to break through ambivalence and progress to the **preparation stage**. Real transformation occurs when individuals identify their own compelling reasons to change, fostering a genuine and sustainable motivation for the journey ahead.

Understanding the stages of change offers valuable insight into your journey of transformation. Let's look at specific exercises you can use to blast through ambivalence so you can finally move ahead.

Exercise 1: Strengthen Your "Change" Talk

- **Focus on language that emphasizes your desire for positive change.** Use phrases like "I want" or "I am committed to" to reinforce your motivation for the desired outcome. Soften the "sustain" talk, which tends to emphasize maintaining the status quo.
- **Replace the word BUT with AND.** Replace the word "but" with "and" to acknowledge and consider both sides of the ambivalence without judgment. For example, if you want to start exercising regularly, you may be thinking "I want to work out in the morning, but I am not a morning person. Try saying this instead, I want to work out in the morning and I am not a morning person. This linguistic shift helps you break free from the trap of all-or-nothing thinking.
- **Practice total acceptance and unconditional positive regard.** Embrace both aspects of your conflicting feelings with unconditional positive regard. Accepting your emotions without judgment forms the foundation for working through ambivalence and moving toward healthier ways of being.

- **Recognize both sides as equally important.** Recognize and treat both sides of your ambivalence as equally important. Avoid favoring one perspective over the other. This balanced approach fosters a more harmonious internal dialogue.
- **Avoid neglect.** Neglecting one side of the conflicting feelings can lead to rebellion. When a part of you feels ignored or dismissed, it may rebel, resulting in a stubborn refusal to move forward, even when it's in your best interest.
- **Befriend both parts.** Instead of viewing conflicting emotions as adversaries, befriend both parts of yourself. Understand that each aspect has valid concerns and desires. This acknowledgment lays the groundwork for a more cooperative internal dynamic, reducing resistance and promoting forward movement.

Exercise 2: Tip the Scale toward a Reason to Change

When we think about making changes, most of us don't really consider all "sides" in a complete way. Instead, we often do what we think we "should" do, avoid things we don't feel like doing—or just feel confused or overwhelmed and give up thinking about it at all. This exercise is useful if you're in the precontemplation or contemplation stage of making a specific change, like giving up alcohol or implementing a new health and fitness routine.

Change is more likely to occur when we come to our own reasons for the change, so the goal of this exercise is to tip that balance. This can help us to hang on to our plan in times of stress or temptation.

Think about the specific change you want to make, and answer the questions below:

- How would you like things to be different?
- What are the good things about ____, and what are the less good things about it?
- When would you be most likely to____?
- What do you think you will lose if you give up ____?
- What have you tried before to make a change?
- What do you want to do next?
- What are the good things about ____?
- How would you improve ____?
- What attempts have you already made to improve your situation?
- What's different now about ____ than when you started?
- How could changing the way you work make things different?
- How have your goals changed?
- What changes would help you achieve your goals?
- How has ____ helped you improve professionally or personally?

Exercise 3: Pros and Cons of Change

Whenever you consider a significant change in your life, you need to explore the pros and cons associated with that change. This process involves bringing hidden ambivalence into the light of day to see a clearer picture, so you can truly evaluate whether the benefits outweigh the potential challenges of enacting the change. By acknowledging and examining these conflicting thoughts and emotions, you open the door to a deeper understanding of the reasons driving your desire for change.

To begin, we need to identify the change under consideration and then carefully list the reasons for and against it. By honestly assessing the pros and cons of your goal, the aim is to convince yourself of the positive reasons for change. This process helps tip the scale in favor of the motivating factors, consolidating the drive to move forward and initiate change.

Change is more likely to occur when you arrive at your own compelling reasons for change. Instead of merely following perceived societal expectations or avoiding uncomfortable tasks, thoughtful exploration of pros and cons helps you make more informed decisions and fortifies your commitment to the plan even in the face of stress or temptation.

With a clear view of the complexities involved, you can make a conscious choice. If, and only if, you decide the change is worth the perceived hassle, you will find the determination needed to propel yourself forward on the path of transformation.

1. **Identify the change.**
    a. Clearly define the specific change you are contemplating, whether it's related to habits, relationships, career, or lifestyle.
    b. Create a list of reasons for making the change, covering both positive and negative aspects.
    c. Break down these reasons into categories like personal growth, happiness, health, and fulfillment.

2. **Identify hidden ambivalence.**

    a. Reflect on any conflicting emotions, fears, or doubts that might be hidden beneath the surface.
    b. Be honest and nonjudgmental about uncertainties surrounding the change.

3. **Bring ambivalence to light.**

    a. Explicitly write down the identified hidden ambivalence, putting these conflicting thoughts and feelings on paper for a clearer understanding.

4. **Evaluate relevant information.**

    a. Assess the overall picture by examining the reasons for and against the change.
    b. Consider potential challenges, benefits, and the impact on various aspects of your life.

5. **Discuss with someone.**

    a. Engage in a conversation with a trusted friend, family member, or mentor.
    b. Share your thoughts, reasons, and hidden ambivalence with them.
    c. Seek their feedback and listen to their perspective on the proposed change.

6. **Reflect.**

    a. Consider the feedback received during the discussion.
    b. Reflect on the insights gained and how they align with your values and goals.

c. Take note of any new perspectives that may influence your decision.

7. **Make the best choice.**
   a. Assess whether the potential benefits of the change outweigh the challenges.
   b. Choose the path that aligns with your values, promotes personal growth, and contributes to your overall well-being.

Exercise 4: Statement of Motivation

Another way to look at pros and cons is to write down a statement about what you want to achieve, identify potential things you need to consider, and then create a vision for what your life will look like if you successfully make the change. Here are some examples.

1. **Statement of Motivation:** "I want to improve my health and fitness."
   a. Something to consider/plan for: Consider the potential sacrifice of time and effort required for regular workouts.
   b. Question: If my change was successful, how would it look?
   b. Goal: Articulate a clear vision of the positive outcomes of improved health and fitness. Consider factors like increased energy, better mood, and long-term well-being.

2. **Statement of Motivation:** "I aim to build a successful real estate business."

   a. Something to consider/plan for: Consider the potential challenges in balancing work and family time.
   b. Question: If your change was successful, how would it look?
   c. Goal: Envision the success of your real estate business, including increased transactions, a growing client base, and financial stability.

3. **Statement of Motivation:** "I want to create a healthier work–life balance."

   a. Something to consider/plan for: Consider the possibility of adjusting your current work schedule.
   b. Question: If your change was successful, how would it look?
   c. Goal: Imagine a balanced life with dedicated time for work, family, and personal pursuits. Visualize reduced stress and enhanced overall satisfaction.

4. **Statement of Motivation:** "I aim to enhance my personal financial management."

   a. Something to consider/plan for: Consider the need for budgeting and financial discipline.
   b. Question: If your change was successful, how would it look?
   c. Goal: Picture a future with improved financial stability, reduced debt, and increased savings.

Overall Goal: By honestly assessing the pros and cons, the aim is to convince yourself of the positive reasons for change. This process helps tip the scale in favor of the motivating factors, consolidating the drive to move forward and initiate change.

Thinking Traps

One major contributor that keeps us stuck when we are trying to change a behavior or adopt a new way of being is all-or-nothing thinking. Cognitive distortions, also known as thinking traps, are subtle, irrational patterns of thought based on our filter. They are insidious because they feel natural. They are hard to detect, so we fall victim to these thinking traps throughout the day. Some of these traps may cause you to feel inadequate and self-critical, assuming the outcome. They might also lead you to compromise your needs and judge yourself and others.

We make assumptions when we don't have enough data about a particular situation or person, and then filter that through a lens of fear. We also fall into the trap of overgeneralizing, which is a form of cognitive distortion, where stereotypes may also play a role. One bad interaction with a colleague, and you believe you will never be able to find common ground with this person. If you find yourself using the terms "always" or "never," you are likely struggling with this thinking trap.

Emotional reasoning is another thinking trap. It happens when we make conclusions about things based on how we feel instead of the facts about a particular person or situation. For example, maybe you gave a presentation at work, and despite your boss praising your work, you assume she secretly hated it because you have imposter syndrome.

All-or-nothing thinking also happens when you see yourself as either perfect or as a total failure. This thinking trap is the root of procrastination because we often feel like we need to be perfect before we take action.

Where do you see these thinking traps showing up in your life? Here are some examples that might resonate:

- "If I can't give this 100 percent of my time and attention, then it's NEVER going to work."
- "I am completely overwhelmed. I ALWAYS feel like this."
- "I need to stop until I have more time to make this PERFECT."
- "It is impossible to keep this diet going now. I'll start again when I can give it my full attention."

Thinking traps render us stuck; they keep us from moving forward and can be paralyzing at times. They set us up for failure because we put incredible pressure on ourselves. Nothing less than perfect is acceptable, so we don't even try. We get caught in the start-and-stop loop. Or we finally get a boost of motivation, but the minute things get hectic or don't feel perfect anymore, we slam on the brakes.

Perfectionists or people who struggle with control issues suffer from thinking traps BIG TIME! But truth be told, if we look at everything through the lens of all or nothing, we will wait forever, and we'll never reach our goals because we will stay stuck. The good news is that once you recognize these thought patterns, you can replace them with more positive, uplifting thoughts that align with your desired outcome. The key is to become aware of these thinking traps. Remember, it's not the situation that causes the emotion; it is the *belief* about the situation that causes us to jump to conclusions.

Alignment

Self-mastery is the desire to continue improving ourselves in a way that aligns with our purpose, which is why we must align that purpose with our goals. To always be in alignment, mentally and energetically, requires a daily commitment to our mental health. There's no shame in seeking professional counseling. Self-awareness is key to our freedom, and it starts with an honest look within. As I would often say to my therapy patients who struggled with depression and anxiety: "We have to feel it in order to heal it."

Another important feature of alignment is practicing humility every day. Look for opportunities to fall on your sword and take extreme ownership of every aspect of your life. The higher we grow, the more important this practice is. It is very easy to get swept up in social expectations, the pressures of making changes, and comparing ourselves to others. But if we can walk in humility while still keeping our heads held high, we will maintain a sense of peace.

I have also found it extremely important to detach from the outcome of my goals and stay super present in the moment. This prevents me from getting wrapped up in the tremendous pressure and anxiety to achieve a certain outcome. As personal demands and responsibilities grow—which they will, if you are committing to developing self-discipline—the ability to keep your mindset in alignment with your purpose (and the energy you seek) becomes increasingly important.

When you think of the type of person you'd like to be or the life you would like to live, first ask yourself how it would feel to achieve those things. And then line that up with the right habits and behaviors so that becomes your energetic point each day.

To be authentically successful, you've got to internalize the *underlying determination* that you're going to be successful over the long term. But you also have to focus your mental energy on today—on being successful right now, in the short term. When we fully accept where we are, we release the internal conflict within ourselves and become the type of person who can handle the change required. To do that means having enough humility to NOT be perfect—to not have all the answers—but to lean in to the discomfort of trying new ways of *being* and *doing* that are in alignment with what you want life to look like. For example, I accept that I am a people pleaser, that I care too much about what people think, and I can get defensive to protect some aspects of my personality. In my personal journey, I was able to start healing that part of myself so I could move toward change in the areas I wanted to move ahead in. That gave me tremendous personal freedom.

Chapter 6

Navigating energetic resistance involves a conscious effort to clarify our desired feelings, establishing a profound connection with the emotional undercurrents that propel us. These feelings serve as the vital fuel for our metaphorical engine, driving our actions and decisions. It's similar to choosing the appropriate fuel for optimal performance. The right type of fuel may include passion, gratitude, and joy—igniting a powerful energy that propels us forward. Conversely, the wrong type of fuel, such as fear or self-doubt, can hinder our progress. By consistently opting for the right emotional fuel, we empower ourselves to embark on inspired actions, creating a harmonious synergy between our aspirations and the energy we invest in pursuing them.

Self-limiting Beliefs

Self-limiting beliefs are the invisible constraints we impose upon ourselves, often born from past experiences or external influences. These restrictive thoughts shape our perceptions, creating boundaries that hinder personal growth and success. Whether rooted in fear of failure, low self-esteem, or societal expectations, these beliefs act as self-imposed limitations, discouraging us from realizing our full potential.

To overcome self-limiting beliefs, we must first recognize and challenge these negative thoughts, and then replace them with affirmations that foster confidence and resilience. By acknowledging and dismantling these mental barriers, we can liberate ourselves to explore new opportunities, embrace challenges, and unlock untapped potential on our journey to self-discovery and fulfillment.

Constantly reaffirming my aspirations allows me to stay in alignment with the energy that will create the reality I want, and I carry that energy throughout the day as if I've already achieved everything I want. I've learned to act like the type of person I want to become until I become that person who is in complete energetic alignment.

In life, we will always experience highs and lows. That contrast is a powerful catalyst for clarity on our path. It is by experiencing the challenges and triumphs that we gain a profound understanding of our desires and priorities. When clarity emerges, we need courage to take radical action, regardless of the potential costs. This courage stems from a commitment to authenticity and a willingness to embrace change. By having the audacity to follow the path illuminated by our newfound clarity, we embark on our transformative journeys—often defying conventional norms and pushing the boundaries of our comfort zones. The willingness to press forward at all costs becomes a testament to the unwavering commitment to our true calling and the pursuit of a life aligned with authentic aspirations.

To fully commit to change, you must confront and understand the origins of your ambivalence. The first step is to acknowledge your subconscious fears and doubts that contribute to the collision of thoughts and emotions. By unraveling these complexities, you can actively work toward resolving your internal resistance, rebuilding your self-confidence, and ultimately embracing change with a newfound clarity and conviction. The transformative power lies in recognizing ambivalence not as a roadblock but as an opportunity for introspection and intentional growth.

Chapter 7
The Procrastinator's Playbook

If you think you're the only person who struggles with procrastination, you're not alone. Most of the population struggles with pervasive procrastination regularly. It's not a character flaw. Often, procrastination stems from a lack of self-regulation skills, which can be learned. We all avoid uncomfortable tasks at one point or another. Anxiety, boredom, frustration, and overwhelm can all cause us to procrastinate as a coping mechanism. As soon as you recognize that procrastination is an emotional-regulation challenge, you can start to fix the problem.

There's another factor at work too. The brain is wired to encourage avoidance of tasks that stir negative emotions, which prompts us to seek relief through distraction and putting things off. The roots of procrastination intertwine two things: a strong drive to succeed and a fear of failure. Procrastination acts as a protective strategy for coping with conflicting emotions, providing temporary relief from stress and tension associated with challenging tasks. As soon as you think, *I'll tackle this tomorrow*, you feel a momentary sense of relief. Of course, once tomorrow comes, you're right back where you started. You need to identify the most significant areas in your life where you tend to put things off, and then take an honest look at how badly this impacts your business and personal life.

What Causes Procrastination?

Procrastination makes sense when you view it as an unintentional response to the subconscious seeking the path of least resistance. Avoiding tasks that the brain deems painful, threatening, or undesirable fulfills an natural need to reduce tension. Sometimes you might avoid uncomfortable tasks entirely; other times, procrastination shows up as overthinking and an attempt to avoid rejection, failure, and even success. But this isn't a character flaw. It's just the way your brain works!

In the realm of the procrastinator's brain, the limbic system, driven by instant gratification, clashes with the prefrontal cortex's focus on the long game. The limbic system, seeking what's easy and fun in the moment, can lead to a decreased attention span, loss of focus, and a preference for tasks requiring minimal mental and emotional effort. The procrastinator's brain further complicates matters by invoking the panic monster—the brain stem—during moments of fear, like when you're up against a hard deadline or preparing for a big presentation. Traits like perfectionism, self-criticism, and a scarcity mindset contribute to this self-sabotaging cycle, which can become locked in, leading to unhappiness and regret.

We are marvelously creative, but that can play against us when we turn that power toward rationalizing why we should put things off. Creative rationalization stems from an instinct to protect ourselves but plays out as subtle sabotage. We might even find ourselves fearing success and failure simultaneously, leading to indecision and paralysis. Overthinking exacerbates the problem, making tasks seem more complicated and challenging than they are. Things like unhealthy sleep patterns, a habit of negative self-talk or self-criticism, a lack of a clear plan, and the plethora of distractions all around us all contribute to procrastination. Luckily, there are tangible, doable steps you can take to kick procrastination to the curb.

How to Break the Procrastination Cycle

Procrastination isn't a problem you have to solve overnight. Instead, you can make simple changes, starting small and building up to bigger ones, to gradually chip away at the procrastination cycle. The first step in changing the procrastination pattern is to recognize the triggers and emotional underpinnings that prompt your need for instant gratification. Procrastination often stems from emotional discomfort such as anxiety, perfectionism, or fear of failure. Reflect on your feelings when faced with a task. Do you feel overwhelmed, anxious, or fearful of not meeting high standards? Recognizing these emotional triggers can help you understand why you might delay starting or completing tasks. For example, if you avoid working on a project because you're anxious about not doing it perfectly, this emotional barrier is a key indicator of underlying procrastination.

How you perceive a task can significantly impact your tendency to procrastinate. If you find tasks to be tedious, overly challenging, or irrelevant, you're more likely to procrastinate. Analyze how you view the tasks on your to-do list. Do you perceive them as too difficult or uninteresting? Understanding your perception can reveal if you're avoiding tasks because they seem too complex or unengaging, which are common reasons for procrastination.

Procrastination can also be a sign of poor time management or prioritization skills. Look at how you plan and allocate your time. Are you frequently distracted or jumping between tasks without completing them? Do you struggle with setting priorities and deadlines? Recognizing patterns in your time management practices can uncover if procrastination is due to a lack of structure or difficulty in organizing tasks effectively.

Once you address the underlying fear that prevents you from tackling certain tasks, you can start to break your habit of rewarding procrastination. Instead, reinforce follow-through by adopting good habits and self-care routines, and rewarding yourself every time you resist procrastination. Here are five common reasons people procrastinate and the underlying fears or avoidance behind them:

1. Fear of failure: People often procrastinate because they fear they won't perform the task well or meet expectations. The possibility of failure can lead to avoidance, as not starting feels safer than starting and failing.

2. Perfectionism: Some avoid tasks because they set impossibly high standards for themselves. The fear of producing something that isn't "perfect" can lead to delay, as they wait for the perfect conditions or mindset to begin.

3. Overwhelm: When a task feels too large or complex, it can create a sense of paralysis. People avoid starting because they don't know where to begin, or feel like they lack the resources or ability to complete it.

4. Fear of judgment: Tasks that involve presenting work to others or being evaluated (like giving a presentation or submitting a project) can cause anxiety. Fear of criticism or negative feedback leads to procrastination as a way to protect themselves from possible judgment.

5. Lack of motivation or connection: Sometimes, people procrastinate when they don't feel personally invested in the task or its outcome. This lack of natural motivation can lead to avoidance, as they struggle to find a reason to start.

Never underestimate the power of your mindset when it comes to procrastination. Self-criticism is never going to boost your motivation. Quite the opposite. Being overly judgmental and harsh with yourself has been shown to hinder progress and increase procrastination. Whenever you feel negative thoughts about failure, try to think about all the times in your past that you succeeded. Have compassion with yourself, and try to become more aware of your feelings so that you can learn to take action despite how that makes you feel.

One of the chief culprits behind procrastination is the lack of a clear plan. As the saying goes, "Fail to plan, plan to fail." Having a well-defined idea of what needs to be done, when the task needs to be done, and how you're going to tackle it helps you focus your efforts. Create to-do lists for each goal you want to accomplish, with specific due dates placed on a visible calendar so that each task becomes a tangible commitment. As you plan out projects and tasks, make sure you set yourself deadlines you can realistically meet. Remember, there's always an internal conflict between the part of your brain that wants instant gratification and the prefrontal cortex's focus on the long game. Tasks that lack immediate consequences tend to get sidelined in favor of instant gratification, but deadlines attach urgency, which helps keep you on track. Strategies like time-blocking provide a structure that minimizes the tendency to push essential activities to the back burner. Break big tasks into smaller, less daunting chunks, and set "mini" deadlines so you can achieve quick wins. This will give you a sense of progress that also boosts productivity. Small victories make you feel accomplished and propel you forward.

Mel Robbins's 5 Second Rule, which I mentioned earlier, can help you get started on tasks. Give yourself a five-second countdown, and then just start. I also love the 5 Minute Rule, which is a technique used in cognitive behavioral therapy where you say, "Okay, I'll do this task, but only for five minutes." We can do anything for five minutes, right? Often, you'll find that by the time five minutes is up, you want to keep going. If you're prone to overthinking or perfectionism, these are powerful tools to help you get things done.

It also helps to focus on one thing at a time, seeing each task through to completion before you tackle the next. I like to set hourly check-ins, to keep tabs on whether I'm staying on track. This also helps me do a better job of planning in the future because I learn how to better estimate how long certain tasks realistically take.

Don't forget to reward yourself when you follow through! It's so important to reinforce positive behaviors. Chronic procrastinators often neglect to acknowledge their achievements, which delays gratification. You can use self-rewards to satisfy your limbic brain's need for instant gratification, while also satisfying your prefrontal cortex's view toward the long term. It's a win-win for your brain. Every time you complete a task, reward yourself with something tangible, if you like, and with positive self-talk. Congratulate yourself and celebrate small wins. Make a habit of self-acknowledgement, and you will unlock powerful motivation.

There's another formidable adversary in the battle against procrastination: the plethora of distractions that surround us. In a world filled with all sorts of ways to satisfy our need for instant gratification, it's easy to get addicted to the allure of novelty. For you, this might show up as "shiny object syndrome," where you get distracted by starting another new project or taking another online course. Distractions not only hinder progress but also provide instant gratification—those dopamine hits that perpetuate the cycle of procrastination. In the next chapters, you'll learn more about how to detox your life from some of these distractions and create new habits to support your newfound understanding of where you struggle and how to make sure you don't slip back into old habits that no longer serve you.

And finally, go back to those foundational self-care routines you learned in Chapter 2. There's a well-established correlation between lack of sleep and diminished levels of willpower, patience, and focus. A well-rested mind is better equipped to handle challenges, make good decisions in the moment, and persist through strenuous tasks. Fatigue fuels procrastination, but good nutrition, exercise, and other self-care routines all contribute to better sleep. Take care of yourself, and you can avoid another stumbling block on the path to productivity and fulfillment.

Above all, remember to give yourself compassion when you stumble. When I was younger, I never gave myself compassion or understanding. I caused myself so much unnecessary pain. This is about *progress*, not perfection! Give yourself grace when you don't achieve a ten-out-of-ten day. Self-compassion alone is a powerful antidote to procrastination. Research shows that self-forgiveness reduces future procrastination, and daily, small, incremental goals make it easier to get quick wins you can celebrate. Combined with a clear plan, fewer distractions, healthy sleep habits, and a deep sense of purpose, you'll be able to break free from the shackles of procrastination and fly toward your goals.

Chapter 8
The Un-Niceties:
A Guide to Embracing Your Inner Rebel

This chapter is about embracing your inner rebel. It's about letting go of societal "shoulds" and the need to always be nice. The more you get to know yourself and learn to release self-judgment, the more you're able to break free from the herd. Yes, you CAN refuse to conform to external standards that don't resonate with your true self! Everything changes when you begin to love and accept yourself—it's like becoming your own magnet for awesomeness.

Recently, during my morning meditation, I came to an unusual awareness that it is not my job to impact other people or make them feel good or comfortable. As a child, I was trained early on to please everyone and make sure I could control the chaos as a way of self-protection. I became a people pleaser at a very young age. My whole life, I have felt like my purpose was to change other people's lives and impact them. Yes, I still have that desire, but I realize that it is nearly impossible to change people or even make them feel good. If I stay in my heart center, living through bliss, I believe my impact on others will just be a natural byproduct of my state of being.

This realization released a lot of pressure that I didn't realize I had put on myself. Living in a way that I thought could change the behavior of others and make them happy meant I often had to compromise aspects of myself. While my intentions may have been pure, it wasn't the right approach.

Listen, it is NOT your responsibility to make others happy.

The Un-Nicety of Being Unfailingly Nice

The societal expectations of being unfailingly nice have inadvertently muted our voices, creating a culture of conformity that stifles authentic expression. While kindness is undoubtedly a virtue, the pressure to maintain constant agreeability can lead to silencing. If we want to reclaim our voices, opinions, and rightful space in the room, we must challenge the notion of never upsetting the apple cart.

Choosing not to be overly accommodating doesn't equate to being unkind. It's about establishing boundaries and expressing our genuine opinions, even if it upsets others. Fear of rocking the boat hinders progress and innovation. Disagreement often fosters a culture of diverse perspectives, which can lead to growth and understanding. Let's not be afraid to challenge the status quo, even if it means upsetting other people on occasion.

Trying to be *nice* is actually fueled by fear and people-pleasing tendencies. These stem from undeveloped thoughts, beliefs, and opinions. Instead, we must express our vulnerabilities with unfettered boldness and determination. Jump into conversations early, speak freely, and trust yourself. Choose truthfulness over perfection. Vocalize your thoughts and beliefs, even if it creates friction. You know yourself better than anyone else, so brush off the negative comments.

In the past, I struggled so much from my constant need for approval. If someone didn't like me, I would be completely crushed. Once I freed myself from the cycle of people pleasing, I felt more connected, more free, and more fulfilled. But in order to do that, I had to boost my internal confidence and self-esteem. I no longer need hardcore proof to validate what my intuition tells me. If something feels off about a person/place/thing, it's because something *is* off. I'm not sticking around to discover what it is. My time and my energy are too valuable for that. I trust my intuition and I *go*.

It takes one hell of a brave individual to piss people off just by merely existing—free, wild, and on your own terms. You deserve to be *you* without judgment, fear, or shame. But if you avoid conflict by trying to be nice and keep the peace, then you start a war within yourself. You can be tolerant and accepting, but tolerance does not mean accepting what is harmful. You're not a doormat. You have the right to set boundaries and enforce them.

There's such a sense of freedom and confidence when you break free from the desire to be liked by other people. Trust that you are a good person, so you do not need to protect or defend yourself against others' opinions of you if they don't like or understand you. Otherwise, you'll spend your entire life seeking external validation and never fully achieving it.

Let Go of the Need for External Validation

On the transformative path to fulfillment, the significance of steering away from a constant yearning for external praise cannot be overstated. Relying solely on external validation is a fleeting and fickle measure of success, and it leaves you susceptible to the whims of other people's opinions. I struggled with this for almost my whole life. Thankfully, my husband is such a great teacher—he constantly reminds me about the importance of being truly authentic and marching to the beat of my own drum. He has also taught me how to be okay with pissing people off if that means I honor my boundaries, do what makes me happy, and speak my truth.

Yes, living authentically and unapologetically can be lonely as you shed people, places, and things that no longer resonate with your highest vibration. The moment it clicked that people do not have to understand me or validate my efforts or success was also the moment I was able to fully understand that I could create the life I truly wanted. I find gratification in the journey, not in external praise or approval.

People—especially those who are insecure with themselves—are always going to question you. They're going to belittle,

Chapter 8

critique, and gossip about you when you're not in the room. But that's going to happen anyway, whether you live a fulfilled, aligned life or you live according to what other people expect. You can never please them.

Wake up every day in perfect alignment with who you are, what you want to accomplish, and the positive impact you want to make on other people's lives. Let the rest go. People are going to come into your life and fall out of your life—that is just the rhythm of a normal life path. Let them judge you; let them misunderstand you; let them gossip about you. Their opinions aren't your problem. Stay kind, committed to love, and free in your realness, no matter what they do or say. Don't dare doubt your worth or the beauty of your truth. Keep shining like you do.

Ask yourself, what do you want your life to look like? And what kind of relationships do you wanna have? Live each day according to what you truly want for yourself.

Stop Shrinking to Fit into Places You've Already Been

Don't hate those who hate you; just ignore them. You can't waste your precious time hating other people. Those who anger you have power over you—remember that. Narrow-minded people blame others, and ordinary people blame themselves, but wise people see all guilt as foolishness. You have to use that truth like medicine and become immune to the haters because the higher you grow, the more hate you may encounter. That's just part of the journey. I like to embrace being disliked as a gift that keeps on giving. It's like a dose of medicine that builds your confidence. When you're being criticized, don't stay quiet. Say something back about your observations of them, not about what they are saying to you. Fire back with calmness but boldness. Stand strong in what you believe and the purpose you follow.

When you are following your bliss, you will inevitably rub others the wrong way and trigger people who are still searching for the same thing as you but haven't found it yet. They may try to pull you off your path or diminish your light, but as long as you are clear and confident in your intentions and your truth, no one can interfere. Radical honesty takes practice. It all starts with loving yourself enough to be completely honest with others and yourself no matter what the outcome is. There is tremendous peace and confidence in knowing that you are better off alone than fitting in with a crowd that is not meant for you.

Success means different things to everyone. When you look outside for approval, remember that you are compromising your integrity. That goes for not only your personal life but your business too. Reserve the right to deny someone your professional services if your soul and spirit don't align with them. The space you share with your soul tribe includes your clients. You don't have to let anyone in just to make money.

Along the road to self-mastery, navigating other people's rejections is like dodging raindrops—you can either grab an umbrella of self-assurance or welcome the downpour

Chapter 8

without missing a beat. You have nothing to prove. Living your true life is not a popularity contest; it's more of a solo performance. Let people be wrong about you. After all, you're not here to win their validation. You're here to master the art of living unapologetically.

Dealing with other people's rejections is a profound lesson in resilience on the journey to living authentically. Other people's opinions, criticisms, or rejections do not define your worth or the validity of your path. Choosing not to be bothered by external judgment is an empowering stance that affirms your unique and personal journey. It is perfectly okay that people will not understand you or accept your choices. I face that daily. I have learned to walk boldly in the direction of my clarity almost like I have blinders on, so I can dial in on my decisions and whatever direction feels inspiring.

Allowing others to be wrong about you is liberating and feeds self-confidence. Letting go of the need to prove your worth to others grants you the freedom to pursue your passions and ideas without being constrained by outside expectations. In the end, living authentically is a journey, guided by your inner compass, your inner navigation system where the opinions of others—especially the ones rooted in insecurity, misunderstanding, and fear—hold no power to derail your path to genuine fulfillment.

Rejection and failure are par for the course. No matter the field or the endeavor, particularly in the sales world, if you are striving to be at the top of your game, you will have to learn how to embrace what's uncomfortable. Sometimes you're going to say, "This sucks!" That's okay. It's not easy to keep going after failure, but it's critically important to be able to do it. It's very easy to feel good when things are going well. It's ten times harder to pick yourself up and keep going after you've been knocked down over and over.

The drive to improve comes from deep within ourselves. Highly accomplished people are paragons of perseverance. They have a ferocious tenacity and vibrant passion for what they choose to focus on. This stems from purpose, determination, and a clear direction.

Keep Your Circle Small

To a lot of people, it looks like I have a big circle of friends, but in actuality, I run in small packs. I am often alone, I keep my circle small, I work in silence, and I know my power. In the pursuit of success, maintaining an intimate circle can be a strategic choice. A smaller circle allows for more focused and genuine connections with those who truly support and understand your goals.

This is a lone performance, not a popularity contest. Working in silence and avoiding unnecessary noise can create a space for concentrated effort and introspection. This deliberate approach has helped me shield my goals from unnecessary distractions, allowing me to channel my energy into meaningful endeavors without the pressure of other people's opinions. The power of silence lies in the ability to nurture personal growth with genuineness, selectively sharing achievements with those who genuinely celebrate you.

Chapter 8

Keeping your circle small and curating relationships that align with your growth is a crucial aspect of personal development and success. As you progress in life, it becomes essential to assess and, if necessary, let go of relationships and elements that no longer serve your highest good. This process involves a conscious effort to cut out toxic behaviors and associations that perpetuate gossip, complaining, comparing, and criticizing. These negative patterns can hinder personal growth and impede your journey toward success. People who habitually criticize others often operate from a place of lack, fear, and insecurity. Surrounding yourself with such influences can adversely impact your mindset and hinder your progress. Recognizing the importance of a positive and supportive environment is imperative for personal success.

It is not just about cutting ties but also about making deliberate choices to bring in positive influences that contribute to your growth and evolution. This might involve reevaluating current relationships, establishing boundaries, and fostering connections with people who uplift and inspire you. Reflecting on which relationships need nurturing and which require boundaries helps you create a supportive network conducive to personal and professional development. The ability to make difficult choices about your social circle is an empowering step. Recognizing when relationships no longer align with your goals, and having the courage to let them go, allows space for new and positive influences to enter your life. Ultimately, the people you surround yourself with play an important role in shaping your mindset, aspirations, and, consequently, your success. You essentially become the average of the five people you spend the most time with, so choose your circle wisely.

Make alliances with winning people, and curate a circle of individuals who strive to do their best and radiate positive energy. This will inspire you to elevate your own standards and work toward your goals. Together, a supportive circle fosters mutual support and encouragement. Positive vibes can be contagious, propelling everyone in the circle toward greater achievements.

Acceptance is a key component of building a winning alliance. While it's important to accept people as they are, it's equally important to place them where they belong in your life. As the CEO of your life, the power to hire, fire, and promote those within your circle lies with you. Surrounding yourself with those who share your values and ambitions and who contribute positively to your journey ensures a more fulfilling and purpose-driven life.

Engaging with people who talk about goals, vision, and ideas also encourages your forward-thinking mindset. It shifts the focus from the trivialities of gossip to the substance of personal and collective growth. By promoting a culture of aspiration and positivity within your circle, you can all motivate each other to strive for excellence and create a ripple effect of success.

Take Extreme Ownership

Taking extreme ownership of every aspect of your life is a hallmark of true winners and high achievers. Regardless of external circumstances or judgments about fault, those who embrace this mindset understand that success and personal

Chapter 8

growth hinge on accepting responsibility for both positive and negative outcomes. This approach transcends the inclination to play the victim in challenging situations.

Real winners recognize that external factors, though influential, do not define their journey. They understand that true empowerment arises from taking ownership of their reactions, their decisions, and the path they forge. Even when faced with adversity, high achievers refrain from casting blame and instead focus on what they can control.

Extreme ownership involves a profound sense of accountability, acknowledging that the outcome of any situation is a reflection of personal choices and actions. It's about looking inward for solutions and improvements, regardless of external circumstances. This mindset not only builds resilience but also fosters a proactive approach to life, where challenges become opportunities for growth rather than excuses.

In essence, embracing extreme ownership is a powerful declaration of agency over one's life. It is an acknowledgment that, regardless of external forces, the locus of control remains internal. This mindset not only propels individuals toward success but also liberates them from the constraints of victimhood, fostering a mentality of empowerment and self-determination. True winners understand that taking ownership is not just a choice; it's a transformative way of navigating life's journey.

Many individuals navigate life like corks in the ocean, reacting to the immediate waves of demands. Conversely, successful people look ahead, holding on to a vision of the future rather than merely trying to get through the day. The stark contrast between those who achieve greatness and those who tread water lies in their ability to resist the pull of reactivity mode.

Many individuals with immense potential may falter because they become entangled in life's distractions, losing sight of their goals. This reactive mindset often stems from indirect motives, diminishing motivation and performance. Emotional pressure, driven by external threats to your identity—such as fear, peer pressure, or shame—diverts focus from the value of the work itself to the external consequences or rewards, creating a detrimental impact on the quality of outcomes.

Success Is an Equal-Opportunity Endeavor

As I mentioned earlier, one of the reasons why I love the challenge of running a marathon is that it's me against myself. Everyone running the race has the same opportunity to succeed. It's the same in business or any endeavor. When it comes to discipline and dedication, we're all on the same playing field. It's not a popularity contest; it doesn't matter how many friends you have on social media or how many people "approve" or accept you. All of that fake superficial shit goes out the window, and your true character and mental toughness are revealed.

Whether you're training for a marathon, building a business, or entering into a new relationship, stop comparing yourself to others! Run the race you are in. That is where you will find happiness and fulfillment. This awareness is so powerful and should inspire you to take control of your life, your goals, and your dreams. Realize that you have a choice every single day to make a different decision, choose a different path, shift your perspective, make amends, clean up your side of the road, so to speak, so you do not have any emotional baggage holding you back and causing distractions for your higher purpose—which is ultimately to live the width and the depth of your life to the fullest.

You have the ability to limit the egoic distractions of comparing yourself to others. Keep in mind that some people may simply be threatened or intimidated by your success. Do not allow them to dim your light or make you question your true power.

In a world of so much distraction, comparison, superficial importance, and the challenges you face running your own race, it's your unique set of standards that help you persist and keep you from getting lost in the Bermuda Triangle of distractions.

Yes, your new life is going to cost you your old one. It will cost you your comfort zone and sometimes your sense of direction. Don't worry. You will develop a new direction, one that is aligned with who you are, and that will not carry you along a path that others expect you to follow.

Your new life may cost you relationships and friends—you won't always be liked or understood. But the people who are meant for you will meet you on the other side. And you're going to build a new comfort zone around the things that move you forward. Instead of being liked, you're going to be *loved*. Instead of being understood, you're going to be *seen*. *Don't let who you are today talk you out of who you are becoming.* Let it all go.

To those of you who are labeled "aggressive," keep being aggressive.

If you're labeled "bossy," keep on leading.

If you're seen as "difficult," keep telling the truth.

To those who are called "too much," keep on taking up space.

If others say you're "awkward," keep asking hard questions.

Do not shrink yourself to make other people happy or feel more secure. Be yourself. You are beautiful that way.

Chapter 9
The New Habit Manifesto

> *Small disciplines repeated with consistency every day lead to great achievements gained slowly over time.*
> —John C. Maxwell

Progress is about becoming superior to your previous self. It is laying your head down at night, releasing any baggage you picked up during the day, setting your intentions for the next day, and waking up as if you must recommit to yourself, your goals, and the life you desire—over and over—until your dreams, desires, and plans start to come true.

Is that something you strive for? Do you strive to become better than you were last year, last month, or last week? To become self-improving, you must be highly teachable; you must put yourself in learning roles whenever possible. Pick an area you want to improve, and lean in as much as possible. Buy books, listen to podcasts, ask questions, and let knowledge mean more to you than praise, attention, or promotion. As an athlete, I learned this skill at a very young age. I learned how to drop the ego, listen to feedback with a growth mindset, and improve myself by applying what I learned from that feedback.

The first step is to stop talking so much and start listening. Tackle a new discipline even if it makes you feel inadequate. Whenever I am uncomfortable, scared, or intimidated—when I feel stretched and pushed to grow—that is how I know I am on the right track.

In this chapter, I want you to discern the habits that hinder your personal growth from those you need to strengthen so that you can align your actions with your desired identity. This involves establishing no-nonsense boundaries and delineating which habits are nonnegotiable to keep, and which ones need work.

Lay the Foundation for Lasting Change

A habit, in essence, is a behavior repeated over and over until it becomes automatic. The significance of habits lies in their profound impact on our self-perception. Ultimately, habits—good and bad—shape our identity and change our behavior. Cultivating healthy habits is important, not just for their direct benefits but also for the positive influence they have on self-confidence and self-esteem, creating a reinforcing loop of positivity. As behaviors become automatic, so do their accompanying beliefs and attitudes.

Chapter 9

However, changing unwanted habits demands time, attention, and unwavering consistency. Many falter in this process because they have unrealistic expectations regarding their capacity for change, and they underestimate how long it takes to achieve meaningful transformation.

The staggering 92 percent failure rate of New Year's resolutions proves my point.[7] Establishing new habits (and ditching old ones) is hard! It's not just about setting goals but about crafting daily rituals that gradually become ingrained in your routine. To succeed, you have to focus. Cutting out distractions enables your mind to channel its energy toward forming new habits. You've already learned how to create a well-structured daily schedule prioritized to your purpose, and you've detoxed your life to limit distractions. You've set HEART goals and learned how to regulate your mindset and emotions to sustain the self-discipline needed to achieve them. You've explored your strengths and weaknesses, and have tools and knowledge to help you blast through ambivalence and procrastination. Now it's time to lay the foundation for lasting change.

The path to your future is intricately woven with the threads of your habits. Recognize that you're not deciding your future directly; rather, you are shaping it through the habits you foster today. Your habits, in turn, become the architects of the destiny you unfold. It's time to stand firm in the choices you make. Refrain from reverting to habits and situations that hindered your evolution. Remind yourself every day of your deeper

---

7. James Clear, "5 Common Mistakes That Cause New Habits to Fail," James Clear, accessed November 12, 2024, https://jamesclear.com/habits-fail.

purpose. What's the "why" that propels you forward? By holding on to the reasons that fueled your decision to move ahead, you reinforce your commitment to positive change. Stay positive about what lies ahead by maintaining steadfast consistency in the transformations you currently embrace. Your choices in this moment are the foundation upon which your future unfolds, so approach them with purpose and resilience.

Small, Consistent, and Slow

The trio of "small, consistent, and slow" encapsulates the essence of habit formation, equivalent to building a mountain with individual pebbles. Creating a new habit is a gradual process, where each small action contributes to the overall achievement. Consistency is the cornerstone, which goes right back to self-discipline. It's not about sporadic bursts of effort but a steady accumulation of powerful moments day after day. Tiny, incremental, regular changes create huge results over time.

Here's an example. If you eat seven apples in one sitting on a Saturday night, you'll probably get a terrible stomach ache. But if you eat one apple every day for seven days straight, you'll reap the nutritional benefits without any negative side effects. Similarly, doing a little exercise every day is far better than sporadic, intense sessions, which will burn you out and maybe even cause injuries. Bad habits have a cumulative effect too. Eating a bag of chips every day for a year may not affect you too much day to day, but over the long term, your health will likely suffer.

Chapter 9

To be consistent in forming habits, you must confront the obstacles that hinder your progress. What stops you from adopting new habits consistently? Momentum is a powerful thing, but you need to identify anything and everything holding you back. Whether that's time constraints, external pressures, or internal resistance, acknowledging these hurdles allows you to plan your time and schedule strategically to mitigate the roadblocks. Habits are built incrementally—each small step contributes to the larger picture. Knowing this empowers you to stay committed to your goals because you know the key to lasting change lies in the power of consistency.

The Breakthrough Point

If you try to melt an ice cube by gradually raising the air temperature around it, nothing will happen until the ice cube reaches a temperature of thirty-two degrees Fahrenheit. *Atomic Habits* author James Clear uses this example to illustrate what he calls the "breakthrough point."[8] When you first develop a new habit, the initial work you put in often doesn't show any noticeable results at first. There's a lag time between when you first initiate sustained effort, and the moment you see tangible results. To the outside world, your breakthrough point might appear as "overnight success." But if you surrender before you reach that threshold, you'll remain stuck in the "valley of disappointment" forever.

---

8. James Clear, Atomic Habits: An Easy & Proven Way to Build Good Habits & Break Bad Ones (New York: Penguin Random House, 2018).

New habits don't yield immediate results, just like heating an ice cube from twenty-five to thirty-one degrees doesn't give you liquid water. All that energy isn't going to waste; it's simply stored until you reach the melting point.

There's a common misconception that success demands colossal actions. This isn't true. I like to think about habits in the same way I think about money: in terms of compounding interest. Albert Einstein once said "Compound interest is the eighth wonder of the world. He who understands it earns it. He who doesn't, pays it." Compounding interest is the hidden force behind the effectiveness of habits in self-improvement too. Often, we struggle to perceive the incremental impacts of our daily efforts because we're fixated on achieving one grand outcome. Going to the gym for three consecutive days might not transform your physique instantly, nor will studying Mandarin for an hour miraculously make you fluent in the language. It's the daily, seemingly insignificant actions that, when compounded over time, yield substantial results.

In *Atomic Habits*, Clear also discusses a critical phase in habit formation that he calls the Plateau of Latent Potential, a concept that expresses how individuals or groups have significant untapped abilities, resources, or opportunities that remain unrealized. Despite having the potential for greatness or success, this potential is never fully developed or utilized, leading to a sense of stagnation, missed opportunities, and unfulfilled promise.

This "plateau" can be caused by various factors, including the following:

1. Fear of Failure: The fear of making mistakes or failing can prevent individuals from taking risks and pursuing their full potential.

2. Lack of Motivation: Without sufficient motivation or drive, people might not push themselves to explore and develop their latent abilities.

3. Environmental Constraints: External factors such as socioeconomic conditions, lack of resources, or unsupportive surroundings can hinder the development of potential.

4. Self-Doubt: A lack of self-confidence or belief in one's abilities can lead to underachievement.

5. Procrastination: Delaying actions and decisions can result in missed opportunities to realize potential.

Overcoming the Plateau of Latent Potential typically involves addressing these barriers, fostering a growth mindset, seeking opportunities for development, and creating an environment that supports and encourages the realization of potential.

Understanding the dynamics of compounding habits is essential for self-improvement. Positive compounding interest comes from actions like consistent workouts and eating at least four cups of veggies every day. Negative compounding interest comes from things like consistent stress, incorporating stress, negative relationships, and compromising your boundaries. Keep a habit scorecard and stay mindful of your pitfalls, and you'll be well on your way to putting the power of compounding interest to work for you.

This Is Your Brain on Habits

Imagine the brain as a sophisticated computer, tirelessly working to optimize processes and make actions more unconscious. Our brains are hardwired to create neural pathways that automate actions, transforming them into routines that require minimal conscious effort. This automation is a fundamental part of the brain's quest for efficiency, constantly seeking shortcuts to reduce cognitive load and preserve mental energy. Habits are intricately woven into the fabric of our daily lives, serving as our brain's efficient solution to streamline tasks and conserve energy.

Self-discipline and healthy habits play a critical role in creating freedom within our lives. If detrimental habits burden you, you'll likely find yourself entangled in the pressures, stress, and overwhelm stemming from unfinished tasks or negative outcomes. But if you nurture self-discipline and healthy habits, you'll find day-to-day life more manageable and less mentally taxing. This frees up mental space that would otherwise be occupied by questioning when and how tasks will be accomplished. With the basics of life and work attended to through your habits, you're free to think creatively, indulge in downtime, and unplug from constant worries and stressors.

Can you see how habits and self-discipline are not constraints but architects of freedom in your life? By automating routine tasks, life becomes more effortless. You have more bandwidth to enjoy meaningful and fulfilling pursuits. Habits not only shape your actions but also liberate your mind from the

Chapter 9

constant burden of unfinished tasks. The result is a greater sense of control, clarity, and creative potential.

Habits take the hard work out of self-discipline, transforming the effort into a subconscious, almost effortless routine. Committing to one positive habit has a cascading effect on other areas of your life.

Neuroplasticity, the brain's remarkable ability to recognize change and form new neural pathways, plays a significant role in our capacity to develop new habits and let go of old ones. The brain is always searching for the path of least resistance. Neuroplasticity implies that our brains can reorganize themselves, adapting to new information and experiences. The idea that "neurons that fire together, wire together" underscores the brain's ability to strengthen connections between neurons engaged in simultaneous activities.[9] This phenomenon forms the basis for habit formation and dissolution.

To sum up this concept, the "reinforcement loop," a fundamental aspect of habit formation, begins with a "cue," an automatic trigger that can be associated with various elements such as location, time, other people, emotional states, or even specific sounds like an ice cream truck (as illustrated in Pavlov's classical conditioning). The "routine" is the subsequent motivational force, involving physical, mental, or emotional behavior triggered by the cue. The brain craves the emotional state associated with the

---

9. A few online sources indicate that Canadian neuropsychologist Donald Hebb first used this phrase in his book The Organization of Behavior (New York: Wiley and Sons, 1949).

anticipated reward. Finally, the "reward" serves as positive reinforcement, signaling to the brain that the routine was successful. Environmental factors, including the smell of donuts or a familiar car ride, contribute significantly to triggering cues within the reinforcement loop. Understanding this neuroplasticity-driven process provides insight into reshaping habits and optimizing behavior through deliberate cues, routines, and rewards.

Identity-Based Habits

In Chapter 4, you learned how to set identity-based HEART goals. Now you're going to learn to create habits based on your identity to support those goals.

In *Atomic Habits*, author James Clear writes, "It is a simple two-step process: Decide the type of person you want to be. Prove it to yourself with small wins."[10] At the heart of identity-based goals are the things you believe in, followed by specific small steps you can take to get to the end results you want.

You can also think about identity-based habits as the systems you use, like time-blocking and setting a realistic schedule, and daily habits like getting up earlier to create more time for important tasks like exercise.

It's possible to become too goal-oriented. Sometimes a goal-oriented mindset can leave you feeling unhappy, unsatisfied, and like you're burning the candle at both ends. Many people

---

10. Clear, Atomic Habits.

Chapter 9

revert back to their old habits once they accomplish a goal. Ultimately, what determines your success over the long term is your commitment to the process—the systems—that will help you get where you want to go. Focus on your systems rather than the goals, and achievement takes care of itself.

Here's another great quote from James Clear: "You do not rise to the level of your goals. You fall to the level of your systems?"[11] This spotlights how important it is to set up good systems and processes rather than focusing solely on the goals. And lasting behavior change requires delving deeper into the belief systems—your current identity—that consciously or subconsciously drive your behavior.

To become a person of self-discipline, the key lies in addressing this fundamental question: "What do I need to believe about myself to achieve this?" Your answer forms the core circle in the bullseye. Next, consider what actions or processes are required to support this new identity (the process circle). Finally, articulate the outcomes you wish to see based on this transformed outlook and identity. This holistic approach emphasizes that changing one's identity and belief systems precedes lasting behavior change, and building supportive systems is key on this transformative journey.

The Laws of Behavior Change

In *Atomic Habits*, James Clear outlines the Four Laws of Behavior Change, which provide key insights into

---
11. Clear, Atomic Habits.

understanding and modifying our habits. If you struggle to match your actions with your goals, such as losing weight, quitting smoking, or starting a new venture, these laws offer a way to address the gap between intention and action. The core idea is that achieving goals depends on aligning our strategies with our natural tendencies. The Four Laws guide us in navigating the complexities of habit formation and disruption.[12]

The 1st Law stresses making good habits visible and integrating them into your environment. For instance, you can enhance your chances of exercising by creating visual reminders, like placing pink tape on your gym equipment, or by incorporating new habits into existing routines through "habit stacking"—such as drinking a glass of water every morning with your coffee. To break bad habits, make them less accessible, and remove temptations from your environment, as it's easier to prevent exposure than to resist it.

The 2nd Law focuses on making habits appealing. Our brains are driven by the anticipation of rewards, so combining a less enjoyable task with a pleasurable one—known as "temptation bundling"—can make the new habit more attractive. For example, allowing yourself to watch your favorite show only while exercising can increase your motivation. Additionally, you can make bad habits less appealing by introducing negative associations, like using bad-tasting nail polish to prevent nail-biting.

---

12. The summary of the Four Laws of Behavior Change that follows in this section are from James Clear's Atomic Habits.

Chapter 9

The 3rd Law involves simplifying habits to reduce effort and friction. The easier a habit is to perform, the more likely it is to stick. This might include preparing for workouts the night before or using the 5 Second Rule to prompt immediate action. Making habits as easy and accessible as possible helps in consistent practice and eventual habit formation.

The 4th Law is about ensuring habits are immediately satisfying. Clear argues that immediate rewards encourage repetition, while immediate punishment discourages behavior. For instance, rewarding yourself with gym time after completing work tasks can create positive associations. Celebrating small successes with immediate, satisfying rewards reinforces the habit and makes it more likely to be repeated.

By applying these principles, you can effectively create and sustain good habits and eliminate bad ones, leveraging the brain's natural inclinations to improve behavior and achieve your goals.

Accountability is key. Try using a habit tracker to track your progress and give you that sense of reward every time you check off the habit from your daily to-do list. Habit trackers help you string together positive behaviors and keep you focused on your journey of self-improvement. Crafting a "habit contract" that incorporates negative consequences for lapses, and having an accountability partner or coach sign the contract, can help to reinforce your commitment. I also love the 5 Second Rule I mentioned earlier, because it stops me from overthinking, prompting immediate action.

And the 5 Minute Rule, because I only have to commit to doing something for five minutes. Usually by the time I'm five minutes into a task, I'm okay to keep going. Next thing I know, the task is done!

You can also leverage technology to help you streamline the process as you build new habits. Tools like Streaks, Loop, Habitify, Productive, and Way of Life cater to your various needs, giving you guidance and prompts along the way and also gathering insightful data about your habits. Employing these proven methods not only reinforces your commitment but also enhances the effectiveness of your new habits and ultimately leads to lasting transformation.

Chapter 10
Grit, Gratitude, Grace, and Finding Peace

The journey of a thousand miles begins with one step.

—Lao Tzu

Living the life of your dreams requires you to step outside of your comfort zone and embrace fear as if it were a sign pointing to your next adventure. It's time to kick it up a notch—whether that means committing to a new challenge, raising the standards for yourself, or simply deciding that average is no longer in your vocabulary. If contentment were a cozy blanket, it's time to kick it off and say, "No more snoozing on the comfy couch of mediocrity!"

That doesn't mean you have to derail your sense of peace in order to achieve big things. This book is about how to live a life of fulfillment. Your higher purpose truly is to live out your greatest potential as a human being in every way possible. To find both peace *and* success on the journey, you need grit, gratitude, and grace.

Because of my silly, goofy, bubbly nature, people have often been surprised by my ability to achieve massive goals in life. I'm the one busting out "the worm" at professional conferences, yet I will be the hardest-working person in the room when it comes down to business.[13] I try not to take myself too seriously. Despite achievements, we are all part of a larger narrative, and the ability to laugh at oneself is a sign of true humility.

The most accomplished individuals often exude lightness and an infectious sense of humor that transcend their achievements. It's this blend of success and simplicity that creates a harmonious life where goals are met with excitement and energy. The laughter shared along the way to the top holds equal importance. **Grit** is the tenacity you need to keep going, **gratitude** allows you to see the lessons on the journey, and **grace** is the art of living simply while achieving greatness. It's a delicate balance that transforms success from a burden to a celebration.

Grit

There's a Japanese proverb that translates roughly to this: "If you fall down seven times, stand up eight." That's been

---

13. The worm, for those who don't know, is a super cool breakdance move from the 1970s and '80s.

Chapter 10

the anthem of my life. Grit has been the backbone of every success I've had, and it is what sustains me through the long, dark journey. As I encounter plot twists in my life and must adjust to a new path I didn't want or didn't foresee—like when I left the world of gymnastics—grit allows me to shift my mindset. It allows me to move forward knowing that tomorrow will be what I make of it.

The authors of *Emotional Intelligence 2.0* aptly describe grit as the "extra something that separates most successful people from the rest." They say it's "the passion, perseverance, and stamina that we must channel to stick with our dreams until they become a reality."[14] Grit goes beyond mere motivation; grit is the backbone of success, embodying the ability to resist short-term gratification for long-term gain. Despite the challenges and hardships on the journey, gritty individuals possess the resilience to press on.

Talent alone cannot guarantee success. You need effort bolstered by grit. The metaphorical thousand-mile journey may begin with a single step, but it's grit that sustains us through the entire expedition, especially in the dark, challenging moments. Elite performers understand the importance of multiple sources of fuel, addressing both physical and psychological needs. This includes adequate sleep, exercise, hydration, and nutrients, along with mental energy derived from curiosity and passion.

Grit manifests as the unwavering attitude of "I won't give up" that characterizes highly successful people. Gritty individuals

---
14. Travis Bradberry and Jean Greaves, Emotional Intelligence 2.0 (San Diego: TalentSmart, 2009).

face challenges head-on and don't back down until they emerge victorious. Their core belief is that the only failure in life is quitting, emphasizing that life is inherently messy and fraught with failures. What truly matters is how one responds to these challenges, and grit provides the tenacity needed to navigate the complexities of the human experience.

At the heart of grit lie essential components such as passion, perseverance, resilience, autonomy, deliberate practice, and a growth mindset versus a fixed mindset. In the realm of self-discipline and success, the ability to persist is the single most crucial attribute. While talent can propel us to a certain point, true achievement demands effort and steadfast follow-through, making grit the foundational element of success.

The enduring power of grit comes from working in alignment with your purpose and passion. That's what enables you to persevere even through the most challenging times. When you are deeply connected to your "why," you're more productive and engaged, and you can perform at a higher level. Willpower, happiness, and motivation are transient, but grit endures through hardships. With grit, you are always able to pick yourself back up and strive for a better tomorrow. Gritty individuals can tune out external judgment and stay true to their unique path.

Gratitude

A big part of my happiness—and I must say, I'm happier now than I've ever been in my entire life—comes from being so grateful. I wake up every single morning and give thanks. I

Chapter 10

am appreciative of the simple fact that I am alive, and that my family has a roof over our heads. I'm grateful that I have the most amazing, loving husband in the world. Whatever happens, gratitude comes first, and the rest takes care of itself.

I don't think people spend enough time being appreciative and showing gratitude. It's easy to take things for granted, and we so often find ourselves chasing something else we feel we lack. That can be exhausting. There's a difference between being grateful and being content. I always say that if I feel comfortable, then I'm not moving forward. When I get comfortable, I know it's time to shake things up with a goal that stretches me.

Gratitude allows us to see the lessons in the setbacks, and to embrace everything that happens along the way as a necessary part of our journey. I truly believe that everything in life gets us closer and closer to our ultimate purpose. We just need the courage to follow it. We have to allow our dreams to be bigger than our fears.

Picture fear as your copilot, not a backseat driver. At any given moment, you have two options: to step forward into growth or to step backward into safety. After all, comfort is the enemy of growth, and what better way to show discomfort who's boss than by giving it a high-five and pressing forward anyway? You cannot fail if you do not give up!

When you come face-to-face with challenges, it's necessary to ask yourself, "What happens when things get hard for me? How do I react?"

In the tapestry of life, remember that your reactions play an integral role in shaping your destiny. While the events themselves may be beyond your control, the way you navigate through them is entirely within your grasp. Each occurrence, whether challenging or serendipitous, is an opportunity for profound self-discovery. Embrace these moments as chances to delve deeper into your understanding and growth.

Grace

I used to be extremely black-and-white in my thought process. This rigid thinking often stems from fear and anxiety. If I didn't succeed at something, I punished myself. But I've since learned to give myself a lot more grace.

This is about progress, not perfection.

Not every day can score ten out of ten. Maybe you're having a five-out-of-ten day right now, and the best thing you can do for yourself at this moment is to lie in bed, watch Netflix, or go for a walk—because that's what you feel called to do, and what you need to reset and refocus. Many years ago, I read a quote somewhere that said to do everything with as much love, gratitude, integrity, and grace as you can—and when you can't, rest instead. We've got to recognize when our body and mind need a break from the race, and give ourselves so much love that we allow ourselves to rest.

In reading this book, I hope you are becoming clear on what your priorities are, and that you will honor your priorities with grit, consistency, and discipline. But when you don't achieve a ten-out-of-ten day, give yourself grace.

When I was thirteen years old, I didn't give myself that grace. Today, I give myself all the compassion and understanding that young Melanie never got. This has allowed me to live a much more abundant, fulfilling, and successful life. In the last five years, I've stepped into real estate full-time and launched an incredible real estate brokerage in Maine, and I feel fortunate that I've had opportunities to coach and teach other agents all over the country. My goal is to inspire, educate, and uplift other entrepreneurs to reach new levels of leadership. But if I'm not living the way I teach, then I'm not doing my job. I want to lead by example.

Finding Peace

Peace comes from a deep knowing that you are more than capable of everything you set out to do. Self-understanding, good habits, and a deep sense of purpose will allow you to reach every goal and dream you aspire to, yet never sacrifice joy along the way. That's true fulfillment.

I'll leave you with some core mantras to guide you on your path to fulfillment:

- Resilience plays a crucial role in navigating the roller coaster of life. Resilience is the willingness to persist when others might give up, coupled with the awareness of when to surrender gracefully. Resilience allows you to soften into the present, making room for what will be. It allows you to ease into a state of flow so that high performance feels almost effortless. As you develop a mindset of curiosity and growth aligned with your values, you move toward this state of optimal performance.

- Aspiring to success is universal, but true determination comes to light when faced with the reality of what it demands. You must have the courage to relentlessly work toward your desired opportunities. Stay hungry and humble, consistently striving to be the hardest-working person in the world while still being generous with self-compassion.
- Peace comes from focusing on gratitude and spending time with those who truly care. Complaining only saps energy. In the social realm, adopt a philosophy of not caring about others' opinions. Take more risks, and choose a lifestyle over just a job.
- Daily exercise not only keeps your body fit but also nurtures a healthy mind. I also recommend you keep a journal to reach for whenever you need to unload, work out conflicting thoughts, self-reflect, and practice gratitude.
- Perseverance is embedded in getting back up after a perceived failure, fixing your ponytail after an ungraceful land, and trying again after initial setbacks. Consistent—not perfect—effort wins the game in the end.
- Setting boundaries is essential for self-respect, and scheduling your time according to your priorities allows you to move forward with a silent determination. Remembering to evolve and embrace growth will keep you grounded in the present, acknowledging the

continuous journey toward becoming a better version of yourself.
- Talent is not the sole determinant of success. It also takes work ethic, passion, and coachability.
- A holistic approach to personal development comes from strength intertwined with gentleness, education with humility, fierceness with compassion, passion with rationality, and discipline with freedom. The importance of listening, being calm, and observing are virtues that lead to effective communication and understanding.

And here are a few steps you can take on your journey to fulfillment:

- If your HEART goals don't make you a little afraid—a little nervous—then the goal is not big enough for you. Clear out the noise. Get centered on your truth—that deep knowing about who you are, who you want to become, and all that you want to achieve in your lifetime. Only you know what that truth is. Everything is achievable with perseverance, passion, and focus.
- Spend some time pondering what every aspect of your life would look like without fear. If you had no fear, what would you do today? What would you do in five years? If you didn't care what other people thought about you, what would you do? What would your health look like? Your bank account? Your relationships?
- Take an inventory of your life now, and again throughout each year. Become obsessed with what is required of you to live the life you are destined to live.

- Do something each day that makes you uncomfortable. That might be making an intimidating phone call, scheduling an interview, or anything else you don't normally do. Whenever I do something that scares me a little, it makes me feel alive! Listen, we don't have time in this short lifetime to be complacent. Each one of us has a gift, and we need to live it through. We think time is on our side, when truly it's not. So if you want to achieve something, whether it's becoming the kind of person you want to become or having the relationship you want to have, it's time to work toward it.

I truly believe I'm here on this planet to help others see their full potential. And I want you to see your true significance, whatever that means to you. Maybe you want to work at Starbucks, or develop your real estate career. Maybe your purpose is to be an amazing mom, teacher, business owner, or artist. It doesn't matter what you *do,* as long as you feel like you are living to your full potential.

Life is kindred to a book composed of various chapters—some filled with sadness, others with joy, and a few brimming with excitement. Each chapter unfolds a unique story, presenting you with opportunities for growth, learning, and transformation. The beauty lies in the act of turning the page. Welcome the uncertainties, and discover the narrative that awaits in your next chapter. Without the courage to explore the unknown, you might miss out on the richness and depth that life's chapters bring. Embrace the journey, turn the pages, and savor the diverse experiences that shape your story.

Take the Next Step

Thank you for taking this journey with me! I hope the insights and strategies shared here inspire meaningful transformation in your life. This is just the beginning; let's stay connected! Follow me on instagram, facebook, and elevatemaine.com for more tools, resources, and updates on how we can continue to grow together.

1. Hire Melanie to Speak
If you are looking for a motivational speaker for your conference, event, or mastermind, I'd love to bring it!
Email: melanie@elevatemaine.com with "SPEAKING" in the subject line.

2. Connect on Social Media
Let's keep the convo going! The journey doesn't end here. I'd love to connect with you on all social platforms. Let's have some fun!
You can find me on Instagram @melaniecraneelevatemaine
Feel free to leave a review!

Acknowledgments

Writing this book has been an incredible journey, and I couldn't have done it alone. I am deeply grateful to my family, who provided emotional support, encouragement, and inspiration throughout the process. You were my rock when I needed grounding and my cheerleaders when I needed a push.

A special thank you to my husband, who not only made sure I was well-fed but also insisted I got a good night's sleep after countless hours pouring my heart into these pages. Your care and attention kept me going in more ways than I can count.

To my coaches and mentors: thank you for challenging me to think deeper, push harder, and never settle. Your insights and guidance have been invaluable.

This book would not have come to life without the incredible team behind the scenes. A heartfelt thank you to Adrianne Dyer for your thoughtful proofreading and editing. Your keen eye was a gift. To Mary-Theresa Tringale, thank you for your unwavering support throughout the process. Tara

Taylor, your editing brought clarity and polish, and Sophia Hanks, your skillful formatting brought this book to life in its final form. Each of you played a vital role in shaping and presenting this work, and for that, I am endlessly grateful.

Thank you to everyone who believed in this project. Your encouragement made all the difference. This book is as much yours as it is mine.

About the Author

Melanie has a diverse background in clinical social work, athletics, and real estate. She consistently demonstrates a commitment to making a difference in the lives of others. Before cofounding Elevate Maine Realty, Melanie practiced exceptional empathy and expertise through working with children and adolescents with PTSD, supporting families, and assisting collegiate athletes with performance anxiety. Her experience ranges from working in local schools and nonprofit organizations to serving in prominent medical facilities like Maine Medical Center. Melanie formally owned and operated her private practice and specialized in offering comprehensive care to those in need.

Melanie's background as a former Division I gymnast provided her with a unique perspective on discipline, determination, and the pursuit of excellence. Her expertise as a cognitive behavioral therapist and also her role as assistant team leader at Maine's largest real estate firm allowed her to gain an even deeper understanding of human behavior and market dynamics. This distinctive blend of talents has led to Melanie's reputation for truly comprehending her clients' needs, going above and beyond to ensure their satisfaction.

Beyond her professional achievements, Melanie is deeply passionate about inspiring the youth in her community. She travels across the country sharing her wisdom on essential topics such as self-discipline, healthy habits, balance, mindset, and grit. Her mission is to uplift and motivate others, encouraging them to discover their true purpose and live life to the fullest. She believes in releasing old patterns, relationships, and narratives to step into one's fullest potential. Her fun, vibrant, loving spirit creates a sense of community wherever she goes, fostering connections and encouraging others to join her on the journey toward self-discovery and fulfillment.

www.ingramcontent.com/pod-product-compliance
Lightning Source LLC
Chambersburg PA
CBHW070152100426
42743CB00013B/2887